CUTTING EDGE

ELEMENTAR

Longman

STUDENTS' BOOK

sarah cunningham   peter moor
with frances eales

WB Exercises to be found in the Workbook

Task and Speaking	Writing	Functions and Situations
Preparation for task: read a document and check information **Task:** use documents to exchange information about two people (speaking)	**Writing:** complete personal details on a form **WB** **Punctuation:** capital letters **WB** **Improve your writing:** addresses in English	**Real life:** giving personal information *Pronunciation:* sentence stress in questions
Preparation for task: listen to someone talking about her family tree (listening) **Task:** Draw a family tree and talk about your own family (speaking)	**WB** **Spelling:** plurals **WB** **Writing:** *People in your family*	**Real life:** classroom English
Preparation for task: identify the topic of short conversations (listening) **Task:** find six things in common with a partner (speaking)	**Writing:** write about the difference between your country and Britain **WB** **Improve your writing:** commas (,), full stops (.), *and* and *but*	**Real life:** telling the time *Pronunciation:* polite intonation
Preparation for task: read an e-mail from Laura and answer questions **Task:** read replies to Laura's e-mail and choose the best e-mail friend for Laura (speaking)	**Writing:** a paragraph about a foreigner who lives in your country **WB** **Improve your writing:** a paragraph about a friend	**Real life:** classroom English
Preparation for task: listen to people answering questions about transport **Task:** prepare and conduct a class survey on transport (speaking)	**Writing:** complete an Internet booking form for train tickets **WB** **Improve your writing:** complete an immigration form	**Real life:** buying a ticket
Preparation for task: listen to someone describing a picture **Task:** ask and answer questions to compare two pictures (speaking)	**WB** **Improve your writing:** Describe food from your country	**Real life:** ordering food and drink
Preparation for task: listen to someone describing different times in her life **Task:** talk to a partner about different times in your life (speaking)	**WB** **Improve your writing:** time linkers	**Real life:** ordinal numbers, dates and years

Task and Speaking	Writing	Functions and Situations
Preparation for task: identify what is happening in some pictures **Task:** use the pictures to invent a story (writing)	**WB Improve your writing:** a diary	**Real life writing:** write a diary in English
Preparation for task: listen to people talking about souvenirs **Task:** decide on the best souvenirs for different people (speaking)	**Writing:** write a paragraph about a market you know **WB Improve your writing:** describe a place	**Real life:** asking in shops
Preparation for task: answer questions about a picture and listen to someone describing it **Task:** add details to a picture then ask and answer questions with a partner (speaking)	**Writing:** write sentences to describe someone **WB Spelling:** ...*ing* forms **WB Improve your writing:** correcting mistakes	**Real life:** street talk
Preparation for task: do a general knowledge quiz and listen and check your answers **Task:** write quiz questions in groups then do a class quiz	**Optional writing:** write questions to test your teacher's general knowledge **WB Improve your writing:** punctuation	**Real life:** different ways of saying numbers
Preparation for task: read descriptions of three places then listen to people discussing plans for a day out **Task:** Plan a day out in groups (speaking and writing)	**WB Improve your writing:** a popular holiday place	**Real life:** talking about the weather
Preparation for task: read three class web pages **Task:** plan a class web page (speaking and writing)	**WB Improve your writing:** a note	**Real life:** telephoning *Pronunciation:* polite intonation
Preparation for task: read an advertisement for a tourist attraction **Task:** advertise a tourist attraction you know (writing)	**WB Improve your writing:** a postcard **WB Spelling and pronunciation:** silent letters	**Real life:** directions
Preparation for task: read about three students **Task:** choose a course for each of the students (speaking and listening)	**WB Improve your writing:** abbreviations on application forms (*Mr, Mrs, Dr, n/a, Tel*)	**Real life:** complete an application form for an English course

(**Language summary** (pages 141–149))   (**Irregular verbs** (page 150))   (**Tapescripts** (pages 151–159))

What English do you know?

1 Common words

Find the pairs of words. Say the words.

1 man – c woman

 1 man
 a listen

 2 boy
 b write

 3 teacher
 c woman

 4 chair
 d window

 5 door
 e girl

 6 look
 f student

 7 open
 g table

8 say
h close

2 Numbers 0–21

Write the numbers with the words.

twenty 20	eight	nine	four ....
sixteen	fifteen	five	ten ....
three	zero	seven	two ....
one	seventeen	twelve	thirteen ....
six	twenty-one	nineteen	
eleven	eighteen	fourteen	

3 Plurals

a) What are the plurals?

1 book books
2 teacher teachers
3 desk ....
4 pen ....
5 chair ....
6 student ....
7 girl ....
8 boy ....
9 man ....
10 woman ....

b) How many can you see in the picture?

five students

4 The alphabet

a) Say the alphabet in English.

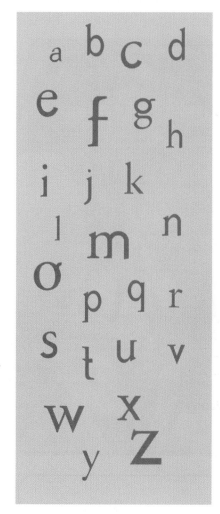

a b c d
e f g h
i j k
l m n
o p q r
s t u v
w x z
y

b) Spell:

- your first name.
- your surname.
- the name of your street.
- the name of your city.

5 Pronouns

Match the pronouns to pictures a–g.

| they | he | I | it | you | she | we |

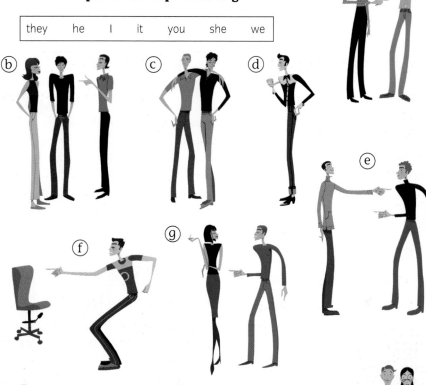

6 Possessive adjectives

Put the words into the table.

| your | his | our | their | ~~my~~ | her |

My teacher!

a I   → my teacher   d she   → .... teacher
b you   → .... teacher   e we   → .... teacher
c he   → .... teacher   f they → .... teacher

7 Numbers 1–100

a) Write the next three numbers.

21   twenty-two, twenty-three, twenty-four

- twenty-one (21)   • sixty-six (66)
- thirty-five (35)   • seventy-four (74)
- forty-three (43)   • eighty-one (81)
- fifty-six (56)   • ninety-seven (97)

b) Say the number then say the number <u>before</u>.

21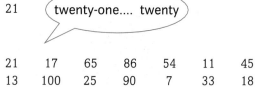
twenty-one.... twenty

| 21 | 17 | 65 | 86 | 54 | 11 | 45 |
| 13 | 100 | 25 | 90 | 7 | 33 | 18 |

module 1
People and places

▶ *be*: positive, negative, questions and answers
▶ Names and countries
▶ *be*: personal questions and information
▶ Articles *a, an*; jobs

Task: find information from documents

Language focus 1

be; names and countries

1 **a)** Match sentences 1–4 with answers a–d.

1 How are you? d

2 What's your name?

3 Where are you from?

4 Nice to meet you.

a And you.

b I'm from England.

c My name's Emily Harman.

d I'm fine, thanks.

b) 🔊 [1.1] Listen and check your answers.

2 Practise this conversation in pairs.

> Hello, my name's ....
> What's your name?

> My name's ....

> Nice to meet you.

> And you.

Grammar

be: questions and answers

you	Where **are you** from?	What**'s your** name?
I	**I'm** from England.	**My** name**'s** Emily Harman.

▶ *Language summary A/B page 141.*

Practice

1 **a)** Walk around the class. Ask and answer these questions.

> What's your name?

> Where are you from?

b) Now introduce a student to the class.

> This is Ramón, he's from ...

> This is Monika, she's from ...

Grammar

be: questions and answers with *he*, *she* and *they*

he	*Where's he from?*
	He's from Milan.
she	*Where's she from?*
	She's from Brazil.
they	*Where are they from?*
	They're from New York.

▶ *Language summary A page 141.*

2 Match these sentences with the pictures above.

a   He's from Brazil.   ☐

b   She's from Britain.   ☐

c   They're from Spain.   ☐

Pronunciation

🔊 [1.2] Listen and practise saying these countries.

• •   • •   •   •• •   • • • •
Brazil   Britain   France   Italy   Argentina

• •   •• •   •   • •••
Japan   Poland   Spain   the USA

3 Point to the pictures. Ask and answer questions like this:

> Where's she from?

> She's from Poland, I think.

9

Language focus 2

be: personal information

1 a) Complete the gaps in conversations 1–3 on the right.

b) 🖭 [1.3] Listen and check your answers.

2 a) 🅼🅳 Match sentences a–k with the people in pictures 1–3.

a He's from Poland. ☐1

b They're from Tokyo. ☐

c They're about twenty-two. ☐

d He's a student at Warsaw University. ☐

e They're tourists. ☐

f She isn't on holiday, she's on business. ☐

g He's nineteen years old. ☐

h They're on holiday in Italy. ☐

i She's about thirty-five and she's married. ☐

j He isn't married, he's single. ☐

k They aren't married, they're friends. ☐

b) 🖭 [1.4] Listen and check your answers.

3 🖭 [1.5] Complete the table in the *Grammar* box. Then listen and check your answers.

Pronunciation

🖭 [1.5] Listen again and practise saying the short forms.

1

A: What's his name?
B: His name's. Jarek.
C: Where'.... he from?
D: He'.... from Poland.

2

A: What's her name?
B: Her name'.... Carmen.
A: Where'.... she from?
B: She'.... from Spain.

3

A: What are their names?
B: Their names .... Toshi and Mariko.
A: Where .... they from?
B: They'.... from Tokyo.

Grammar

be: positive, negative and short forms

➕	short form	➖	short form
I am	I'm	I am not	I'm not
you are	you're	you are not	you aren't
he is	....	he is not	....
she is	....	she is not	....
it is	it's	it is not	it isn't
we are	we're	we are not	we aren't
they are	....	they are not	they aren't

▶ *Language summary A page 141.*

Practice

1 a) Make four **true** sentences and four **false** sentences about the people on page 10.

b) Test your partner. Your partner corrects the false sentences.

> Toshi's from Tokyo.

> True!

> Toshi and Mariko are married.

> False! They aren't married, they're friends.

2 Read sentences a–j. Tick (✓) the ones that are true. Correct the false ones.

a You're in an English lesson. ☑

b You're from China. ☐
   I'm not from China, I'm from Hungary.

c You're from Italy. ☐

d Your school's in New York. ☐

e Your classroom's very small. ☐

f Your teacher's from Scotland. ☐

g Your teacher's married. ☐

h Your father's a politician. ☐

i Your parents are from the USA. ☐

j Your English lessons are in the evening. ☐

Language focus 3

be: personal questions

1 Tick (✓) the correct answer to questions 1–6.

1 Are you a student?
a Yes, she is.
b No, they're on holiday.
c Yes, I am. I'm at London University. ✓

2 Where are you from?
a I'm a student.
b We're from Australia.
c I'm on business.

3 How old are you?
a I'm fine, thank you.
b He's about thirty-two.
c I'm twenty-one.

4 Are you married?
a Yes, we are.
b No, they aren't. They're friends.
c No, I'm on holiday.

5 Are you on holiday?
a No, I'm from Brazil.
b Yes, I am.
c No, they aren't.

6 What's your job?
a I'm an architect.
b I'm from Italy.
c I'm a tourist.

2 🔲 [1.6] Now listen to the conversations and check.

Grammar

1 Questions with *be*

Notice the word order:

*How old **are you**?*

***Are you** married?*

*What'**s your** job?*

***Is your** teacher American?*

2 Short answers to *yes/no* questions:

Are you married?

   *Yes, **I am**.*

   *No, **I'm not**.*

Is she American?

   *Yes **she is**.*

   *No, **she isn't**.*

▶ ***Language summary A page 141.***

Practice

1 Put these questions into the correct order.

a 's/name/your/what?

   What's your name?

b married/you/are?

c old/you/how/are?

d you/are/how?

e your mother/old/how/is?

f job/your/what's?

g your teacher/married/is?

h your father/old/how/is?

i student/you/are/a?

j your teacher/from Britain/is?

k you/are/on holiday?

l the USA/you/are/from?

m your teacher/old/how/is?

2 Choose seven questions to ask a partner.

Language focus 4

Indefinite articles: *a, an*; jobs

1 Match the jobs with the pictures.

> an actor/an actress   a doctor   a manager   a waiter
>
> a police officer   an engineer   a musician
>
> a sportsman/a sportswoman   a teacher   an artist

2 Ask and answer questions about the pictures in pairs.

> What's his job?

> He's an engineer.

Grammar

With jobs we use the articles *a/an*.

an + vowel (*a, e, i, o, u*)   ***a*** + other letters

*He's **an** engineer.*   *I'm **a** waiter.*

*She's **an** actress.*   *He's **a** police officer.*

▶ ***Language summary C page 141.***

Practice

1 a) Read about a famous person on page 134, 136, 139 **or** 140.

b) Work in groups. Ask and answer questions to find who your partners read about. (Do not ask '*What's his/her name?*')

> Is it a man or a woman?

> How old is he?

2 Play again. This time you think of the famous people.

Real life and writing

Giving personal information

a First name: ....Bruno....

b Surname: ....

c Address: .....Newton Road,....

.....Leeds.....

d Age: ....

e Telephone Number:
....

f Married / Single

g Job: ....

1 [MD] [▭] [1.7] Listen to two conversations then complete the information about Bruno.

2 [▭] [1.7] What questions did you hear? Listen again and complete the gaps.

a How .....old....... are.....you......?

b .... married?

c ....' .... job?

d ....' .... address?

e What' .... number?

f ....' .... your ....?

g .... do .... spell it?

Pronunciation

1 [▭] [1.8] Listen to these questions. Notice the stress.

What's your name?

What's your job?

What's your address?

What's your surname?

What's your first name?

What's your phone number?

How do you spell it?

How old are you?

2 Listen again and practise.

3 Interview another student and complete the information below.

a First name: ....

b Surname: ....

c Address: ....

....

d Age: ....

e Telephone number:
....

f Married / Single

g Job: ....

4 **a)** Read the sentences about Bruno. Find **four** mistakes and correct them.

His name's Bruno Sertori, and he's an actor from Leeds, a city in England. His address is 19c, Newton Road, and his telephone number is 906 0297. He's twenty-five years old and he isn't married.

b) Write similar sentences about a student in your class.

Find information from documents

This is your
NHS medical card
Please keep it in a safe place. It is proof that you are entitled to NHS treatment.
Your NHS Number is
480 320 1639

Your local Family Health Services Authority (FHSA) is
COLCHESTER

Surname   Slater

Forenames   Nicola Rachel

Address   21 Chapel Street Colchester C02 7AR

Tel. no.   (Home) 01206 439094   (Work) ....

Date of Birth   12.06.79

Country of Birth Britain

Marital Status   Married ☐   Single ☑   Widowed ☐
                Divorced ☐

Your doctor is

Dr Shah (4777)
Bradbury Medical Centre
186 Elm Road
Colchester C02 9JG
Tel. 01206 382029

Useful language

Questions

"What's her full name?"

"How do you spell it?"

"What's his (*e-mail*) address?"

"What's her job?"

"What's his telephone number?"

"How old is he?"

"Where is she from?"

"Is he married?"

Other useful phrases

"I don't know."

"Sorry? I don't understand."

Preparation for task

Look at Nicky's medical card. Mark the sentences *Yes* (✓), *No* (✗) or *Don't Know* (?).

a   Her full name is Nicky Slater.   ☒

b   She's British.   ☐

c   She's from Colchester.   ☐

d   She isn't married.   ☐

e   Her telephone number is
    01206 382029.   ☐

f   She's twenty years old.   ☐

Nicky

Task

Chrissie

Jim

1 a) Work in pairs, Student A and Student B.

Student A: Look at Chrissie's documents on page 133. Complete the table about Chrissie.

Student B: Look at Jim's documents on page 134. Complete the table about Jim.

	Chrissie	Jim
Full name		
Age		
Address		
Job		
Where from?		
E-mail address		
Telephone number		
Married / Single?		

b) Student A: Ask Student B questions about Jim. Write the information in the table.

Student B: Ask Student A questions about Chrissie. Write the information in the table.

Look at the *Useful language* box.

▶ *Useful language*

Do you remember?

1 **Write the questions.**

a) My name's Elizabeth. What's your name?

b) I'm fine, thanks.

c) We're from Britain.

d) She's about thirty-five.

e) No, he's single.

f) Their names are Jeff and Rachel.

g) I'm a doctor.

2 **What are the countries?**

a) Br i t a i n   e) S _ _ _ n

b) J _ p _ _   f) _ r _ z _ l

c) P _ l _ _ _   g) A _ g _ _ t _ _ _

d) _ t _ _ y

3 **Short forms: put ' in the correct place.**

a) Shes married. She's married.

b) Theyre from England.

c) Were police officers.

d) Mike isnt twenty-one.

e) The full names *Music Television* (MTV).

f) Im not a teacher.

g) Its 707 4932.

4 **Pronunciation: mark the stress.**

actor   manager   doctor   politician

artist   sportsman   musician   teacher

engineer   sportswoman

5 **Write short answers to these questions.**

a) Is your school big?   Yes, it is .

b) Are you married?   No, ...

c) Is John from England?   No, ...

d) Are you an engineer?   Yes, ...

e) Is your e-mail address
   samwest@BST.co.uk?   No, ...

module 2

You and yours

Language focus 1

this, that, these, those

⌨ [2.1] Circle the correct word (*this, that, these* or *those*) in conversations a–d. Then listen and check your answers.

It's a spoon.

What's *this/that* in English?

This is/That's Marco, my new boyfriend.

Who's *this/that*, over there?

What are *these/those*?

I don't know!

Oh yes, thanks!

Are *these/those* your things, Charlie?

Grammar

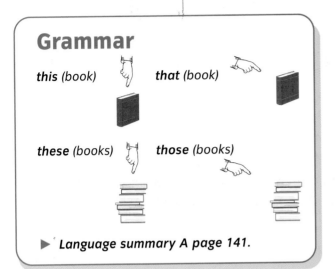

this (book) 👆   that (book) 👉

these (books) 👇   those (books) 👉

▶ **Language summary A page 141.**

Pronunciation

1 📼 [2.2a] Listen to the pronunciation.
this /ðɪs/   these /ði:z/   that /ðæt/   those /ðəʊz/
Practise the four words.

2 📼 [2.2b] Listen to the pronunciation of these questions. Practise saying them.
- What's this?   • What's that?
- What are these?   • What are those?

3 Practise conversations a–d on page 16 with a partner.

Practice

1 Find the objects in the pictures on the left and test your partner.

> a credit card   keys   a camera   a rubber
> an apple   a mobile phone   photos   a diary
> a postcard   a comb   a bottle of water
> a watch   a phone card   a dictionary
> sweets   an identity card

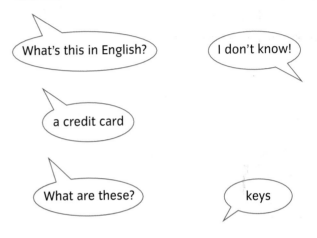

What's this in English?

I don't know!

a credit card

What are these?

keys

Pronunciation

1 📼 [2.3] Listen to the stress in these words:
apple   rubber   photos
camera   diary   dictionary
postcard   phone card   credit card
identity card   bottle of water   mobile phone

2 Practise saying the words.

2 Point to things in the classroom and ask your partner.

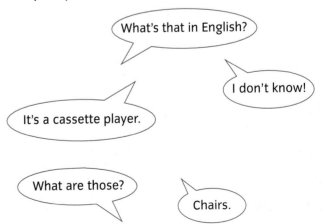

What's that in English?

I don't know!

It's a cassette player.

What are those?

Chairs.

Language focus 2

have got

1 Work in pairs. Say **three** things that you've got with you and **three** that you haven't got with you.

> I've got a pen, a diary and a comb, but I haven't got a mobile phone, a dictionary or a watch.

2 Work with a new partner. Guess what your partner has got in his/her pocket or bag.

> Have you got a dictionary with you?

> Yes, I have. Here it is!

> No, I haven't, it's at home ...

3 Tell the class about your partner.

> Paolo's got a mobile phone in his bag, but he hasn't got a pen!

Grammar

1 Complete the gaps.

➕ **I've got** a new computer. **She's got** blue eyes.

➖ We **haven't** .... a car. He .... a brother.

❓ .... you **got** your passport?

.... **it got** a name?

2 Notice:

He's American. (= he **is**)   **He's got** an American car. (= he **has**)

▶ *Language summary E page 142.*

Practice

1 Complete the gaps with the correct form of *have got*.

a 'Have you got the time, please?' 'Yes, it's 7.30.'

b I think her parents are rich: they'..... .... four cars!

c 'I'm sorry – I ....'..... .... a pen with me.' 'Here you are – I'..... .... two.'

d We'........ .... a new pet dog – his name's Fang!

e '.................... the children .... a new video?' 'Yes, it's great!'

f Anne'..... .... a very big family – six brothers!

g '.................... Paul .... a new motorbike?' 'Yes, it's a Honda.'

2 a) Match questions 1–5 with answers a–c and complete the gaps.

1 .... you got a car?
2 Where .... it from?
3 What make .... it?
4 .... old is it?
5 What .... is it?

a From Italy.
b Very old – about ten years old!
c Red.
d It's a Fiat.
e Yes, I have.

b) Use questions 1–5 to ask your partner about the things in the box. Then write sentences like this:

Paul's got a motorbike. It's a Honda and it's two years old.

| a car | a TV in your bedroom | a moped | a computer |
| a DVD player | a bicycle | a mobile phone | a personal stereo |

Reading and listening

My favourite thing!

1 ☐ [2.4] **MD** Look at the pictures. What are Annie's, Matt's, Ed's and Lucy's favourite things? Listen and read to check your answers.

'This is my car ... it's a convertible, an American car. It's great! It's very comfortable and it's got a brilliant CD player! White is my favourite colour, so it's perfect for me.'

Annie

'My favourite 'thing' isn't really a thing – it's our pet cat, Milly. We've got four cats in my family, but Milly's my favourite. She's black and white, and she's got beautiful eyes. She isn't very friendly to other people, but she loves me!'

Matt

'I'm a professional musician, so my trumpet's really important to me. Actually, I've got three, but this one's my favourite: it's a Bach trumpet made in America – and it's about forty years old!'

Ed

'I've got a fantastic new computer ... I love it! It's a beautiful colour, blue, and it's got games, a DVD player, internet ... in fact it's got everything!'

Lucy

2 Read and discuss in pairs.

a **What is: ...**
- blue?
- very comfortable?
- American?
- new?
- about forty years old?

b **Who is: ...**
- black and white?
- a musician?
- about eighteen?
- not very friendly?

c **Who has got: ...**
- three trumpets?
- four cats?
- beautiful eyes?
- an American car?

d **What has got: ...**
- games?
- a CD player?
- a DVD player?

3 Complete these sentences about each person's favourite things. Cover the text!

a **Annie:** Her favourite thing is her .... It's .... and it's got ....

b **Matt:** His favourite 'thing' is his .... She's .... and she's got ....

c **Ed:** He's got three .... His favourite one is from .... and it's ....

d **Lucy:** Her favourite thing is her .... It's .... and it's got ....

Language focus 3

Family vocabulary and possessive *'s*

1 🔲 Look at the pictures. Do any of the pictures show:

- a husband and wife?
- a mother and son?
- an aunt or an uncle?
- friends?
- a father and daughter?
- parents?
- a brother?
- a sister?
- a baby?
- a boyfriend and girlfriend?
- cousins?
- a grandmother and grandchildren?

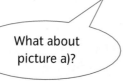

What about picture a)?

I think she's his girlfriend.

2 🔲 [2.5] Were you right about the relationships? Listen to some possible answers. Are your answers the same?

Minnie and Mickey

Grammar

Mickey is Minnie's boyfriend.

We say *Mickey's girlfriend* and *Minnie's boyfriend.*
We don't say *'the boyfriend of Minnie'.*

▶ **Language summary F page 142.**

Pronunciation

1 🔲 [2.6a] Listen to the three ways we pronounce the final *'s'.*

/s/	/z/	/ız/
a Bart's mother	b The Queen's husband	c Astérix's friend

2 🔲 [2.6b] Listen and practise. Is the *'s'* **in bold** like a, b or c?

Minnie**'s** boyfriend   Mike**'s** wife   Paul**'s** daughter   Chris**'s** brother

Practice

1 a) Write five true sentences and two false sentences about the pictures.

Stella is Paul's granddaughter. (false)

b) Read your sentences. Can other students find the false ones?

The Simpson Family

The British Queen and her family

Princesses Stephanie and Caroline of Monaco

Astérix and Obélix

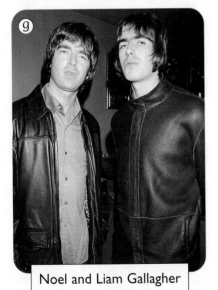

Noel and Liam Gallagher

Paul and Stella McCartney

Real life

Classroom English

1 Read the conversations and tick (✓) the best reply.

1 TEACHER: How do you spell 'cousin' ... Simona?
   STUDENT: a) C-O-U-S-I-N ☑
            b) She's fine. ☐

2 STUDENT: Can you write that, please?
   TEACHER: a) Yes, of course. ☐
            b) No, thank you. ☐

3 STUDENT: Excuse me, how do you say this word?
   TEACHER: a) I understand. ☐
            b) Just a minute, let me see ... it's 'brilliant'. ☐
   STUDENT: Thank you.

4 TEACHER: What have you got for Number 3?
   STUDENT: a) That's right. ☐
            b) I'm not sure. ☐

5 TEACHER: OK, everyone, open your books at page twenty.
   STUDENT: a) Sorry? I don't understand. ☐
            b) Sorry, I don't remember. ☐

   TEACHER: Open your books at page twenty.

2 🔲 [2.7] Listen and check your answers. Cross out the wrong answers.

Pronunciation

🔲 [2.7] Listen again and practise the conversations. Copy the voices on the recording.

3 Now practise the conversations with a partner.

Complete a family tree

Preparation for task

1 Look at Hannah's family tree. Find Hannah.

a Who is John? Who is Sally?

b Is Hannah married? Is John married?

c Who are Marc and Lily?

d Who is Marc and Lily's father?

2 📼 [2.8] Listen to Hannah talking about her family and write the extra information from the box in the right place.

from France	48	baby of the family	
not married	Elaine	a student	Pat

Task

1 **a)** Make a family tree for your family. Write in the names of **six** people.

b) Decide which extra information you can give about each person. Don't write it down!

Ask your teacher for any words or phrases you need.

2 **a)** Work in pairs. Show your family tree to your partner. Tell your partner about your family and answer any questions.

▶ *Useful language a)*

b) Ask questions about the people on your partner's family tree.

▶ *Useful language b)*

John
a ....

b ....
teacher

c ....
very nice!

Serge
d ....

Hannah
...me!...

Marc
f ....

Useful language

a   Your family tree

"This person is my uncle."

"She's (*five*) years old."

"He's (*not*) married."

"I've got (*two*) cousins."

"I'm an only child."

"His wife's name is (*Sarah*)."

"Their names are (*Richard*) and (*Jo*)."

b   Asking questions

"Who is this?"

"How old is (*Lisa*)?"

"What's (*Julia*)'s job?"

Sally

e ....

Lily

g ....

Do you remember?

1 Make five groups of words from the box.

> beautiful   cousin   red   comfortable   television
> cassette player   ~~blue~~   grandfather   coffee
> brilliant   sweets   CD player   white   bottle of water   aunt

a) black ..blue.. ....

b) computer ....

c) important ....

d) apple ....

e) wife ....

2 **a)** **Put the words in the correct order to make questions.**

1) do/spell/How/you/'beautiful'?

   How do you spell 'beautiful'?

2) Sylvia/a/Has/brother/got ?

3) your/is/from/camera/Where ?

4) you/identity card/Have/your/with you/got ?

5) mean/does/'brilliant'/What ?

6) say/do/word/this/How/you ?

b) **Match answers a–f with questions 1–6.**

a) Yes, I have. Here it is.

b) It's Japanese.

c) B-E-A-U-T-I-F-U-L

d) 'Mobile'.

e) No, she hasn't. She's an only child.

f) It means 'very, very good'.

3 Complete the gaps.

a) My father is my mother's husband .

b) My mother's mother is my ....

c) My mother's brother is my ....

d) My sister is my father's ....

e) My mother and father are my ....

4 What does 's mean?

a) What's this in English?   is

b) Ken's got a new bicycle.

c) Mary's on holiday in New Zealand.

d) Gordon's teacher is from India.

e) Jo's address is 7, Park Road, Birmingham.

module 3

Something in common

► **Vocabulary:** common verbs
► **Present Simple:** questions, (*I, you, we, they*)
► **Present Simple:** positive and negative (*I you, we, they*)

Task: find things in common with your partner

2 ▭ [3.1] Listen and check your answers to Exercise 1. Practise saying the phrases.

3 ᴹᴰ Add these words and phrases to the verbs in Exercise 1.

| classical music | | in a house | German | Law |
| in a flat | coke | chocolate | | |

Vocabulary

Common verbs

1 ᴹᴰ Write the correct verb in the circles.

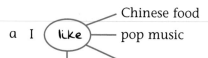

| speak | ~~like~~ | drink |
| study | live | |

a I (like)— Chinese food / pop music

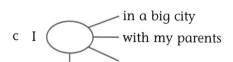

b I ◯— English / French

c I ◯— in a big city / with my parents

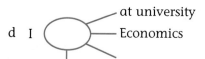

d I ◯— at university / Economics

e I ◯— coffee / tea

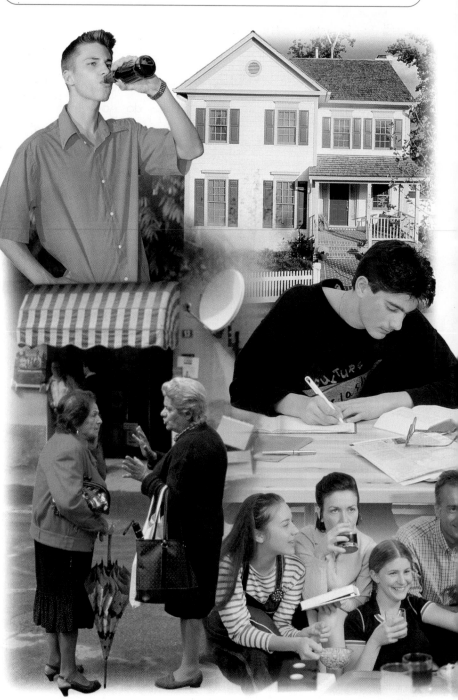

Language focus 1

Present Simple: questions

1 📼 [3.2] Listen to the questions and tick (✓) the answer that is true for you.

a	Yes, I do. ☑	No, I don't. ☐
b	Yes, I do. ☐	No, I don't. ☐
c	Yes, I do. ☐	No, I don't. ☐
d	Yes, I do. ☐	No, I don't. ☐
e	Yes, I do. ☐	No, I don't. ☐
f	Yes, I do. ☐	No, I don't. ☐

2 📼 [3.3] Listen to the questions and answers. Complete the gaps.

a Do you live in .a. big. city?

Yes, I live in ....!

b Do you like ....?

....., ... I love .....!

c .... study at university?

....., I work in a bank.

d .... Italian?

No, I don't, but I .... very well.

e ..... you .... with your .... ?

Yes, I ..... .

f .... tea?

No, but I ....

Grammar

Present Simple with *I*
I live in Tokyo.   *I speak Spanish.*

Present Simple questions with *you*
Do you speak Italian?

Short answers:
Yes, I do.   *No, I don't.*

▶ *Language summary A page 142.*

Pronunciation

📼 [3.3] Listen again notice the stress on important words.

Do you live in a big city?   *Yes, I live in Tokyo.*

Do you like chocolate?   *Yes, I love it!*

Do you...? /djə/ is very weak in the questions.

Practise saying the questions and answers.

Practice

1 Work in pairs. Ask your partner the questions in Exercise 2 above.

2 **a)** Look back at the phrases in Exercise 1 on page 24. Think of **five** questions to ask other students.

b) Walk around the class and ask your questions.

Silvia, do you live in a flat?

No, I don't. I live in a house.

Luc, do you study Economics?

Yes, I do.

Language focus 2

Present Simple: positive and negative

1 ^{MD} Find five pairs of words.

1 start	a in the evening
2 a big meal	b gardens
3 in the morning	c close
4 houses	d finish
5 open	e a snack

2 a) Read the text and complete the gaps with a word or phrase from Exercise 1.

b) ▭ [3.4] Listen and check your answers.

> ## Grammar
>
> **Present Simple: *I, you, we, they***
>
> ⊕ *They **live** in houses.*
> ⊖ *They **don't close** for lunch.*
>
> ▶ *Language summary A page 142.*

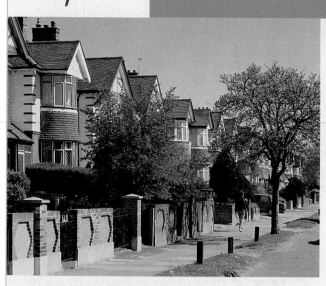

Life in Britain...

Homes and families

Many British people live in (a) ...., not flats. Most houses have gardens.

Daily life

Most office workers (b) .... work at about nine in the morning and finish at about five or six (c) .... Most people don't go home for lunch.
People usually eat a big meal in the evening; they just have a (d) .... at lunchtime.

School life

Children start school at about nine, and (e) .... at about half past three.
Most children have lunch at school.
All children (f) .... school when they are four or five years old, and leave when they are sixteen or eighteen.

Shops and restaurants

Most shops (g) .... at about nine and (h) .... at about six. Usually, they don't close for lunch.
Many supermarkets stay open twenty-four hours. Most pubs and restaurants close at about eleven o'clock.

Practice

1 Complete the sentences for your country. Use either the negative or the positive form.

Most people don't live in houses. They live in flats.

> # Life in
> ## my country...
>
> A Most people .... (live) in houses.
>
> B Most people .... (have) gardens.
>
> C Most office workers .... (start) work at 9.00.
>
> D Most people .... (go home) at lunch time.
>
> E Most people .... (have) a big meal in the evening.
>
> F Children .... (go to school) in the afternoon.
>
> G Most children .... (leave school) at sixteen.
>
> H Most shops stay .... (open) twenty-four hours.
>
> I Most shops .... (close) for lunch.
>
> J Restaurants .... (close) at eleven in the evening.

2 **a)** Compare answers to Exercise 1 with a partner.

b) Write **five** sentences about the differences between your country and Britain.

In Britain, children start school at about nine o'clock in the morning, but in Argentina they start school at...

Real life

Telling the time

1 [3.5] It's four o'clock in London. Listen and mark the times around the world on the clocks.

Los Angeles

São Paulo

London

Moscow

Tokyo

Auckland

> ## Grammar
>
> **Prepositions of time**
> *one o'clock **in** the morning*
> *three o'clock **in** the afternoon*
> *seven o'clock **in** the evening*
> *twelve o'clock **at** night*
>
> Notice: we say **at** *six o'clock*.

2 Match the times with the watches.

twenty to eleven
quarter past eight
five past six
twenty-five past three
half past nine
ten to four

3 **a)** 🔊 [3.6] Write down the times you hear in column A.

b) Complete column B.

	A	B
a	five to ...twelve...	..11..55
b	quarter past	15
c	twenty to	40
d	half past	30
e	quarter	....
f	five	....
g	ten	....
h	half	....
i	twenty-five	....
j	....	....
k	....	....

4 (Circle) the times in a–d. Practise saying the times.

a

BARCLAYS BANK PLC

BRANCH 20-24-61 01
CROYDON 3

BALANCE AT CLOSE OF
BUSINESS ON 10/04/00

1246.71

WITHDRAWAL £100.00

TIMED AT 11.10 ON
11/04/00

b

```
ORG W/ML BREAD
BEER            0.85 9
NEW/C/G/SOUP    5.95 1
                1.79 9

THIS TRANSACTION WILL BE
CREDITED TO YOUR HOME
STORE ACCOUNT

You were served by QUEENIE

GOODBYE, HOPE TO SEE YOU
AGAIN SOON

10/04/00 12:05 1358 000 19666
```

c

Ritzy

♿ **Coldharbour Lane**
American Beauty (18)
(Sam Mendes) 6.35pm,
(Fri/Sat), **Boys Don't Cry**
(18) (Kimberley Pierce)
1.10pm, 3.40pm, 6.10pm.
Star Wars Episode 1: The
Phantom Menace (U)
(George Lucas) Tue/Thur,
10.30am

d

CHANNEL 4

6.00 Friends
PM The One set at the Beach, Rachel is
jealous of Ross. (R) (s)   562
Another Friends episode is on Wednesday
at 6pm

6.30 Hollyoaks
Zara is questioned about the fire. Dan
blames Nikki for their troubles.   814
HELPLINE: for advice on issues raised in
tonight's episode, call free on 0800 500 000.
Lines are open 7–9pm tonight, 9am–9pm
tomorrow

7.00 Channel 4 News
With Jon Snow and Kirsty Lang.
Weather (s)   698611

7.55 Films this week
8.00 Billy Elliot The story of a young boy
from the north of England who learns to
dance.

5 🔊 Ask and answer the following questions in pairs.

a What time do your English lessons start and finish?

> They start at about five o'clock in the evening and they finish at half past six.

b What time do banks open in your country?
What time do they close?

c What time do you get up, usually?
What about on Sundays?

d What time do you come home from work/school?

e What time do you usually go to bed?
What about at weekends?

f What time does your family have dinner, usually?

Find things in common with your partner

Preparation for task

1 ^{MD} 💿 [3.7] Listen to seven short conversations. Number these topics in the order you hear them 1–7.

- ☐ nationality
- ☐ where they live
- ☐ married or not
- ☐ brothers and sisters
- ☐ jazz
- ☐ their ages
- ☒ breakfast

2 💿 [3.7] Listen again. Tick (✓) the topics if the speakers have something in common. Write a cross (✗) if they are different.

3 💿 [3.8] Listen and complete the gaps. Then practise saying the phrases.

1 R...............?
2 .... too!
3 .... neither.
4 How .... you?
5 No, ...

Useful language

a Asking questions

"Are you *married?*"
"Are you *(at university)?*"
"Do you *(live in a city)?*"
"Do you *(like skiing)?*"
"Have you got *(any brothers or sisters)?*"

b Telling the class

"Both of us *(live at home).*"
"Maria lives *(in a city).*"

Task

1 Work with a partner. Write **ten** questions for another student. You can ask about:

- family
- married?
- school/university
- job
- where she/he lives
- likes/dislikes
- age
- languages

▶ *Useful language a)*

2 Work with a new partner. Ask and answer your questions. Find **six** things in common. Use the phrases in Exercise 3.

3 Tell the class **three** things you have in common.

▶ *Useful language b)*

Do you remember?

1 Which words are missing from the following sentences?

a) My wife and I ..live.. in a big house in Washington.

b) Simon and Carina .... to school at 8.30.

c) We .... Law at Manchester University.

d) Do you .... tea with milk?

e) What time do you .... lunch?

f) Do your children .... English?

2 The following sentences have mistakes. Correct them.

a) Jessica and I really like/dog. *dogs*

b) Do you live in Tokyo? No, I don't live.

c) I no speak English.

d) What time people finish work in your country?

e) Wayne and Carla live in Miami?

f) Do you like pasta? Yes, I like.

3 Put a word from the box in the correct place to complete the following sentences.

(in   at   with   do   the   ~~to~~)

a) It's quarter/three. *to*

b) Do your cousins live their parents?

c) What time you have lunch?

d) I usually go home at about 11 night.

e) We've got an English lesson at 8.30 in morning.

f) My sister and her family live the city centre.

4 Are the sounds in bold the same (S) or different (D) in the sentences?

a) Shops close at **ha**lf **pa**st seven. (S)

b) '**Where** are you?' '**We're** here.'

c) We **li**ve at **fl**at number three.

d) I **lo**ve **lu**nch. It's my favourite meal!

e) We've got **four** **Law** students in our class.

f) I like **goo**d French **foo**d.

Now practise reading the sentences.

5 Draw the time on the clocks.

a) half past two   b) seven o'clock

 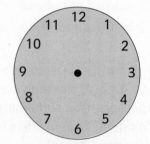

c) quarter to nine   d) twenty past eleven

 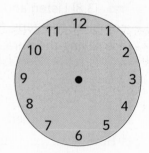

e) half past twelve   f) five to four

 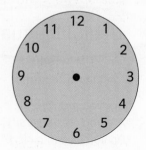

g) quarter past eight   h) twenty-five to ten

30

module 4

Loves and hates

▶ Present Simple: *he* and *she*; like *...ing*
▶ Present Simple questions: *he* and *she*
▶ Activity verbs and adverbs of frequency

Task: find an e-mail friend

Language focus 1

Present Simple *he* and *she*; *like ...ing*

1 a) Who are the people in the pictures? What are their jobs?

b) [MD] Guess who ...

- likes doing housework?
- hates flying?
- loves dogs?
- loves playing golf?
- doesn't like crowds?
- hates television?

2 [4.1] Listen and check your answers **without** reading.

3 a) Complete gaps a–k in the text with the words in the box.

Does	doesn't like	hates
doesn't travel	stops	has
likes	~~loves~~	likes	like
hates		

b) [4.1] Listen again and check your answers.

American superstar **Whitney Houston** (a) ..*loves*.. dogs. She (b) .... two dogs who live in a $75,000 dog house in her garden!

Actress **Kim Basinger** (c) .... crowds – she also (d) .... open spaces!

Sylvester Stallone – star of the 'Rocky' films (e)........... playing golf so much he sometimes (f) .... filming for a game!

Hollywood actress **Cameron Diaz** (g) .... TV.

Actor and film director **Harrison Ford** says he really (h) .... doing housework!

(i) .... Superman (j) .... flying? Well, Actor **Dean Cain** – Superman in the TV series – (k) .... by plane ... he's too nervous!

Grammar

1 Present Simple: *he* and *she*
She loves dogs.　　　　*She doesn't like crowds.*

2 Notice: We use **verb + ...*ing*** after *like/hate/love*:
*He **likes** do**ing** housework.*　　*He doesn't **like** flying**.*

▶ *Language summary A/B/C pages 142 and 143.*

31

Practice

1 Test your partner. Without looking at the text on page 31, make sentences about each famous person.

> Kim Basinger

> She hates crowds.

2 **a)** Match pictures 1–13 with these words.

> playing computer games   spiders   flying
> coffee   running   salad   cats   walking
> swimming   crowds   doing housework
> cooking   pasta

b) Ask your partner what she or he likes and doesn't like. Use the ideas in the pictures to help you.

> Do you like cooking?

> No, I don't – I hate it !

> It's OK.

> Yes, I love it.

3 Use the information below to write about yourself.

> I love ....
> (food/drink)
>
> I also like ....
> and ....
> (activity/sport)
>
> I think ....'s ok.
> (activity/sport)
>
> I don't like ....
>
> I hate ....
>
> NAME ....

4 Take another student's information and read it to the class. Don't read the name! The other students guess who it is.

> This person loves Italian food. She also likes playing tennis and watching football. She doesn't like spiders. ... Who is it?

Language focus 2

Present simple questions: *he* and *she*

1 Would you like to live in another country? Which country?

2 Read about Emma. Ask and answer the questions in pairs.

a Where is she from?
b What is her job?
c Where does she live?
d Does she like it?

An Englishwoman in California...

Twenty-four-year-old Emma comes from Manchester, in the north of England, but now she doesn't live in England; she lives in the United States. Her apartment is near the beach in Santa Rosa, California. 'It's fantastic,' she says 'I go swimming every morning.' Emma is an actress; she lives in Los Angeles because it's near Hollywood, the home of the American film industry. 'I love the way of life here,' she says 'It's a beautiful and exciting place ... the weather's really good – it doesn't rain very much, like at home! – the people are open and everyone looks so good! The only problem is that people think my accent is strange ... when I speak to taxi drivers, sometimes they don't understand me!'

An American
in England...

3 🔊 [4.3] Listen to an interview with Bob Kessler and answer the questions.

a Where is he from?   c Where does he live?

b What is his job?   d Does he like it?

Grammar

1 **Present Simple questions:** *he* and *she*
   *Where **does he** live?*
   ***Does he** like it?*

2 **Short answers:**
   *Yes, he **does**.*   *No, he **doesn't**.*

▶ *Language summary D page 143.*

Practice

1 **a)** Make questions about Emma on page 33.

1 Emma/live in England?
   Does Emma live in England?

2 she/like going to the beach?

3 she/like life in the United States?

4 it/rain a lot in California?

5 Emma/speak with an American accent?

b) Now make five questions about Bob.

1 Does Bob live in England?

---

c) Ask and answer the questions from Exercise 1a) and b) with a partner.

> Does Emma live in England?

> No, she doesn't.

2 **a)** Think of a foreigner who lives in your country: a friend, a famous person or perhaps your teacher! Write a paragraph about the person like this:

My friend Rita comes from Amsterdam in the Netherlands, but now she lives in my city, Madrid. She works in a shop in the morning, and in the afternoon she teaches English to small children. She loves life in Madrid. She thinks the restaurants and nightlife are fantastic, and she likes the weather. There's only one problem, she says; in July and August it is very, very hot here! She loves life in Madrid, and she says Spanish people are very friendly.

3 Work in pairs. Ask your partner questions about their person like this:

> What's his name?

> His name's David.

a What's his/her name?

b What's his/her job?

c Where does he/she come from?

d Where does he/she live?

e What does he/she like about your country?

f What does he/she think of the weather?

g What does he/she think of the people?

Language focus 3

Activity verbs and adverbs of frequency

1 🔲 Put the verbs in the box in the right place in the circles.

> play   listen to   write   watch

a) **read** — a newspaper / ....

b) **go** — swimming / ....

c) ⬭ — football / ....

d) ⬭ — a letter / ....

e) ⬭ — the radio / ....

f) ⬭ — television / ....

g) **go to** — school / ....

h) **visit** — friends / ....

2 **a)** 🔲 Add these words to verbs a–h above.

> shopping   a magazine   an e-mail   the guitar
> CDs   a video   the cinema   your grandparents

b) It is important to remember words that often go together. Practise saying the phrases above. Then test your partner like this:

> play

> play the guitar ...
> play football ...

3 **a)** Put the adverbs in the right place on the line.

> ~~always~~   usually   often   sometimes
> not...often   ~~never~~

100% ←—————————————————→ 0%
always   never

b) Which sentences are true for you?

1 I often go shopping on Saturday. ☐
2 I always read the newspaper in the morning. ☐
3 I never watch football on television. ☐
4 I don't often write letters. ☐
5 I usually listen to the radio in the car. ☐

Grammar

Word order with adverbs of frequency
He **never** watches football on television.
I **always** read the newspaper in the morning.
I **don't often** listen to the radio.

▶ *Language summary E page 143.*

35

Practice

1 Look at the activity verbs on page 35 again. Write a sentence about something:

a you never do.

I never listen to the radio.

b you don't often do.

c you sometimes do.

d you often do.

e you usually do at the weekend.

f you always do in the evening.

2 a) [MD] Work with a partner. Ask and answer these questions:

Do you ever ...

- **play tennis?**
- **visit your grandparents?**
- **watch a video at the weekend?**
- **read poems?**
- **go swimming in the sea?**
- **watch television in the morning?**
- **listen to jazz music?**
- **go to school on Saturday?**
- **read magazines?**

Do you ever visit your grandparents?

Not often ... how about you?

b) Write **four** sentences about your partner.

Jarek never reads magazines.

Find an e-mail friend for Laura

Preparation for task

Laura wants to find new friends on the Internet.

Read what Laura writes about herself in her e-mail and answer these questions:

a Where is Laura from?

b Is she a student?

c How old is she?

d Does she like music?

e Does she enjoy reading?

f Does she have any other hobbies?

New Message - 1

Send Address Attach Reply Reply All Forward Draft Print Delete   ☒ Log ☐ Receipt   Normal ▼

Hi! My name's Laura. I'm from Greenock, a town in Scotland. I'm a student at Glasgow University – I study Spanish and French – and I'm twenty-one years old. I love music of all kinds (both writing and playing – I play the piano, the guitar and I write songs too); I also like going to the cinema, reading, computers … and dogs! I love writing and receiving e-mails, and I hope to make friends with people all over the world. Please write!

Task

1 Laura gets replies from four people. Work in pairs, Student A and Student B.

Ariel from Argentina

Johanna from Sweden

Peter from Singapore

Rachel from the United States

Student A

a) Ask questions to Student B about Ariel and Johanna. Write the answers in the table.

b) Look at the information about Peter and Rachel on page 140. Answer Student B's questions.

Student B

a) Look at the information about Ariel and Johanna on page 139. Answer Student A's questions

b) Ask questions to Student A about Peter and Rachel. Write the answers in the table.

▶ *Useful language a)*

2 **a)** Who is the best e-mail friend for Laura? Put the people in order, 1–4.

Ariel ☐   Peter ☐
Johanna ☐   Rachel ☐

b) Discuss your answers with other students in the class.

▶ *Useful language b)*

Useful language

a Asking for information

How old is *(Ariel)*?

Is he/she a student?

Does she like *(music)*?
Does he play *(the piano)*?
Does she speak *(German)*?

What does he/she like doing?

Have you got any other information about him/her?

b Talking about the best e-mail friend

I think *(Ariel)* is good because he speaks *(German)*.
I don't think *(Rachel)* is good because she doesn't like *(music)*.

	Ariel	Johanna	Peter	Rachel
age?				
student?				
likes? (*music, reading, animals*)				
plays (*the guitar, the piano, football, tennis*)				
speaks (*English, Spanish, German*)				
other information?				

Reading and vocabulary

1 MD Check the meaning of the words in the box.

> a traffic jam   a journey   wait   crowded

2 🔊 [5.2] Read the text and put the numbers from the box in the gaps. Then listen to the recording and check.

> 1,000,000 (one million)   25   3   53,000,000 (fifty-three million)
> 59   100,000,000 (one hundred million)   5

factfile factfile factfile factfile factfile

Transport facts!

○ Traffic jams in Bangkok, the capital city of Thailand, are so bad that a normal journey to work takes about (a) .... hours!

○ People in most countries drive on the right – but people drive on the left in (b) .... countries, including Japan, India, Australia and Great Britain.

○ More than (c) .... people in the world ride a bicycle!

○ Every day, more than (d) .... people travel into the centre of London: 35% go in by underground, 30% take the train, (e).......... % travel by car, 7% catch the bus, and 3% walk to work!

○ In Tokyo, people never wait for more than (f) .... minutes for an underground train. The only problem is that the trains are so crowded that it's difficult to get on – or get off!

○ (g) .... people fly to and from O'Hare Airport in Chicago, USA every year! (That's about one hundred people every minute!)

factfile factfile factfile factfile factfile

3 a) Look back at the text and choose the correct words to go together.

1 *drive/~~ride~~*   a car
2 *drive/ride*   a bicycle
3 travel *with/by*   car
4 fly *in/to*   Chicago
5 *wait/wait for*   a bus
6 get *on/in*   a train
7 get *off/out*   a train
8 walk *to/in*   work
9 *ride/take*   a train

b) Test your partner like this:

drive → drive a car

4 Make sentences that are true for your town or country. Compare your answers in small groups.

In ....

a most people *drive very fast/ drive very well/don't drive very well.*

b *not many people/some people/ a lot of people* ride bicycles.

c traffic jams *are a big problem/ are sometimes a problem/ aren't a problem.*

d the buses are *very crowded/ not very crowded.*

e you *often/sometimes/never* wait a long time for a bus.

f people *often/don't very often/ never* fly from one city to another.

g people *always/usually/never* wait in a queue to get on and off buses and trains.

▶ *Language summary A page 143.*

Language focus 1

Articles : *the*, *a*, *an*, and zero

Look at the pictures and read about Carl Wilson. <u>Underline</u> the articles *a*, *an* and *the*.

Carl Wilson is 35 years old. He's an artist, and he lives in Boston, a large city in the United States.

b) 🔲 [5.3] Listen and check your answers.

Grammar

1 When do we use *an* instead of *a*?

2 Is there usually an article with names?

3 Which article goes with which group (*a*/*an*, *the*, zero Ø)?

a *I've got a new car, I live in a big city.*   .a.

b *she's ... teacher, ... tennis player, ... doctor.*   .....

c *in ... morning, in ... afternoon, in ... city centre.*   .....

d *in Ø. Paris, in Ø New York, in Ø Spain.*   .....

e *in ... United States, in ... UK.*   .....

f *by ... bus, by ... car, by ... train.*   .....

g *go ... home, go to ... school, go to ... work.*   .....

h *on ... Friday, on ... Saturdays.*   .....

▶ *Language summary B page 143.*

Practice

1 **a)** Read what Carl Wilson says about transport problems in his city. Complete the gaps with *a*, *an*, *the* or zero (Ø).

I live near (1) ...the... city centre, and we have (2) .... real problem with cars here. Most people come to (3) .... work by (4) .... car, so in (5) .... morning when people drive into (6) .... Boston, and in (7) .... evening, it's very busy. I have (8) .... car, but I don't drive much; I'm (9) .... artist, so I usually work at (10) .... home!

2 Answer the questions using a phrase with *a*, *the* or zero (Ø).

Quiz

a **Write five ways to go home from your school.**

b **When do most people...**
get up?
have breakfast?
go home from work?
watch TV?

c **What are these people's jobs?**
Kate Winslet
Ricky Martin
Martina Hingis
Tony Blair

d **Which day of the week do people usually...**
go to church?
eat out?
watch football?
stay at home?

Do a class survey on transport

Preparation for task

1 Read the survey below and check any words or phrases you don't know.

2 🖭 [5.6] Listen to people answering the questions. Which question does each person answer?

Person A = Question .....S.....   Person D = Question ....
Person B = Question ....   Person E = Question ....
Person C = Question ....   Person F = Question ....

Task

1 Work in groups of three or four. Write two more questions for the survey.

2 Use the survey to interview each other.

Useful language

Asking questions

"Do you use *(the bus)*?"

"How far do you *(walk)*?"

"How do you *(go to town)*?"

"How long does it take?"

"What do you think of *(public transport)*?"

Answering questions

"Yes, *often/sometimes/ every day.*"

"No, *never*".

"About *(five) kilometres/ minutes/hours.*"

"By *train/bus/bicycle.*"

"I walk to *(the city centre).*"

TRANSPORT SURVEY

Your personal transport

1 Do you ...
drive a car? ○   ride a motorbike? ○
ride a bicycle? ○   ride a scooter? ○

2 How far do you walk in a normal week?
0–1 kilometres ○   1–3 kilometres ○   4–5 kilometres ○
more than 5 kilometres ○

Public transport

3 Do you use public transport
every day? ○   often, but not every day? ○   sometimes? ○   never? ○

4 What do you think of the public transport in your town or city?
Excellent ○   Good ○   I don't know ○   other

Your journey to school/work

5 How do you go to school or work every day?
by car ○   by bus ○   I walk ○   other ○

6 How long does it take?
1–5 minutes ○   5–15 minutes ○
15–30 minutes ○   more than 30 minutes ○

Real life and writing

Buying a ticket

Florence is in London. She wants to travel to Paris.

1 Read the conversation in a ticket office and put it in the right order.

☐ Here you are.

☐ Platform eighteen.

☐ Single.

☐ Single or return?

☐ Thanks. Which platform is it?

☐ That's £49.50, please.

☐ A ticket to Paris, please … the six o'clock train.

☐ Thank you. Sign there please.

| Home | Browse Timetable | Book Your Ticket |
| Destinations | Services & Facilities | |

Ticket Order Form

Send ticket(s) to

Person 1

Name as on passport: Mr or Ms ....

Address ....

City .... Country ....

Phone ....

e-mail ....

Person 2

Name as on passport: Mr or Ms ....

Tickets

Ticket ordered

Depart City .... Date .... Time ....

Arrive City .... Date .... Time ....

Click on (1st) CLASS or (Standard)

Number of Persons ....

Here is my CREDIT CARD INFORMATION

| Registration | 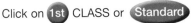 Contact Us |

2 🖭 [5.7] Listen to the conversation and check. Then practise the conversation in pairs. Change:

• the city.

• the cost.

• the ticket (single/return).

• the platform number.

3 **a)** You can also buy a train ticket over the Internet. You want to catch the train to Paris. Decide:

• who you want to travel with.

• where and when.

b) Complete the order form.

module 6
Eating and drinking

> ▶ **Vocabulary:** food; countable and uncountable nouns
> ▶ *There is* and *there are*
> ▶ *Some* and *any*
> ▶ *How much?* and *how many?*
>
> **Task:** describe the differences between two pictures

Vocabulary

Food: countable and uncountable nouns

1 Look at the meal in a hotel. Is it breakfast, lunch or dinner?

2 Find these things in the picture.

milk	coffee	fruit juice	cereal	fruit
bananas	apples	oranges	~~cheese~~	meat
~~eggs~~	toast	bread rolls	~~butter~~	jam
yoghurt	biscuits	grapes	sausages	

3 a) Put the words in the box into two groups:

things you can count (countable nouns)

- .eggs..
- ....
- ....
- ....
- ....
- ....
- ....
- ....

things you can't count (uncountable nouns)

- cheese
- ....
- ....
- butter
- ....
- ....
- ....
- ....
- ....

b) Can uncountable nouns have a plural form?

▶ *Language summary A page 144.*

48

4 🔊 [6.1] Listen to three people talking about what they have for breakfast. Write down what they have.

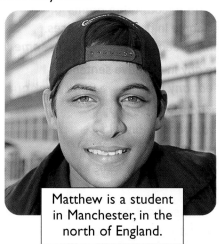

Matthew is a student in Manchester, in the north of England.

Sonia comes from Recife, in the north of Brazil.

The Weber family live in Germany.

5 What do you usually have for breakfast? Tell your partner.

For breakfast I usually have …

Language focus 1

There is and *there are*

🔊 [6.2] Listen to the sentences about the picture on page 48. Are they true or false?

a ..True....   b ....   c ....   d ....
e ....   f ....   g ....

Grammar

Circle the correct answers to complete these sentences.

Singular: *There's/There are* a jug of milk.
Uncountable: *There's/There are* a lot of cheese.
Plural: *There's/There are* eight bread rolls.

▶ *Language summary B page 144.*

Practice

1 Look back at the picture on page 48. Write four **true** sentences and four **false** sentences about the things in the picture.

There are eight bread rolls. ✓

There are seven oranges. ✗

2 Work in pairs. Test your partner using your sentences. Your partner closes his/her book and corrects the false sentences.

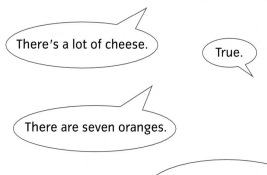

There's a lot of cheese.

True.

There are seven oranges.

False – I think there are about four oranges.

Listening

'Waiter! Waiter!' Jokes

1 [MD] Find the meaning of these words, and match them to one of the pictures a–c.

| cherry | surprise | feathers | fly | ice cream |

2 [6.3] Listen to three jokes. Which joke goes with which picture?

(a)

(b)

(c)

3 Write the last line of each joke. Check your answers.

JOKE 1

Waitress: Do you want a cherry on top?
Customer: No, ...

JOKE 2

Waiter: Oh yes, you're right.
.... a knife and fork, sir?

JOKE 3

Customer: So, what's the surprise?
Waiter: .... , sir!

4 [6.4] Look at the joke below. Fill the gaps with a word or phrase from the box. Listen and check.

| you're | sir | on | can |
| ~~waiter~~ | a | it | see | there |

Customer: Waiter!
(1) *Waiter!*.
Waiter: Yes, (2) .... ?
Customer: (3) ....'s
(4) .... spider in my soup!
Waiter: Really, sir?
(5) .... I see?
Customer: Look! There
(6) .... is!
Waiter: Oh, I (7) ....
Yes, (8) .... right sir.
The fly is (9) .... holiday.

Real life

Ordering food and drink

1 Look at pictures 1–3 on page 53. Which restaurant sells:

a pizzas?   b hamburgers?
c coffee and cakes?

2 [6.5] Listen to three conversations.

a Which of the three restaurants are they in?
b What do the people order?
c How much does it cost?

3 Listen again and complete the phrases with words from the box. Practise with a partner.

can	anything	away
else	have	keep
what	order	much

4 Work in pairs, Student A and Student B.

Student A: Choose something to eat and drink from the menu. Order your food!

Student B: Take Student A's order. Tell him/her how much it costs.

C = CUSTOMER   W = WAITER

(from Conversation 1)

w: Can I take your order, please?

c: (1) .... I have two super King-Size Burgers, please.

w: (2) .... to drink with that?

w: Eat in or take (3) ....?

(from Conversation 2)

w: Would you like anything (4) ....?

c: Can I (5) .... the bill, please.

c: (6) .... the change.

(from Conversation 3)

c: I'd like to (7) .... a pizza – to be delivered, please.

w: (8) .... would you like?

c: How (9) .... is that altogether?

menu

Breakfast

croissant and jam	1.40
fried eggs and tomatoes	1.20
sausages and eggs	1.05

Burgers

king size	2.35
classic	2.10
with cheese	2.50

Cakes · homemade ·

chocolate	1.50
coffee	1.50
apple	1.75

Drinks

tea	55	hot chocolate	90
coffee	70	coke	80
cappuccino	1.40	orange	80

Sandwiches

tuna mayonnaise	2.20
egg mayonnaise	1.99
cheese	1.99

Extras

chips	1.80
salad	1.80
bread	1.50

Describe the differences between two pictures

Preparation for task

⌨ [6.6] **Listen to someone describing the picture. Put a number in the circle next to the part of the picture she describes.**

Useful language

a Describing your own picture

"In my picture …

there's a *(small dog)*."
there are some *(potatoes)*."
there aren't any *(apples)*."

"On the left/on the right/in the middle, there's …"

b Asking questions

"In your picture, is there a *(cat)*?"

"Are there any *(oranges)*?"

"How many *(potatoes)* are there?"

"How much are the *(bananas)*?"

"What colour is *(the cat)*?"

c Talking about differences

"In Picture A *(there's a cat)*, but in Picture B *(there isn't)*."

"I haven't got any *(apples)* in my picture."

"In his/her picture there's *(a dog)* there isn't *(a cat)*."

Task

1 a) Work in pairs. Do not look at your partner's picture.

Student A: Look at Picture A on this page.
Student B: Look at Picture B on page 135.

b) There are **eight** differences between the two pictures. Find them by describing your picture and asking questions. Mark the differences on the picture.

▶ *Useful language a) and b)*

Do you remember?

1 Write the missing letters to make seven food and drink words.

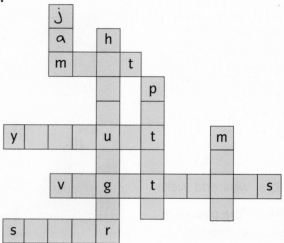

2 Tick (✓) the sentences that are true and change the ones that are false.

a) There are twenty students in my class.
No, there aren't. There are twenty-five students.

b) There are two railway stations in town.

c) There's a university in town.

d) There's a computer room in the school.

e) There are three children in my family.

f) There's a beach near my home.

3 Write the questions, using *how much* or *how many*.

a) How .... meat/you/eat in a week?
How much meat do you eat in a week?

b) How .... fruit/you/eat?

c) How .... sugar/you/have with your coffee or tea?

d) How .... hours' sleep/you/have at night?

e) How .... time/you/work on a computer every day?

4 Make five groups of words with the same sounds.

| eggs | wife | milk | meat | juice | healthy |
| cheese | grilled | spoons | ~~fried~~ | | |

a) knife ....fried.... ....

b) bread ....

c) fish ....

d) cream ....

e) fruit ....

2 a) With your partner describe the differences between the two pictures.

▶ *Useful language c)*

b) Compare answers with the class. Did you find all **eight** differences?

module 7
Extraordinary lives

- ▶ Past Simple: *was* and *were*
- ▶ Past Simple: regular and irregular verbs
- ▶ Vocabulary: past time phrases

Task: tell a life story

Language focus 1

Past Simple: *was* and *were*

1 Why were the people in the pictures famous?

2 a) 🔊 In pairs <u>underline</u> the correct answer.

Icons of the last century

a The artist Pablo Picasso was *French/<u>Spanish.</u>*

b The 1970s group Abba were from *Germany/Sweden.*

c Franz Kafka was a famous *musician/writer.*

d From 1994 to 1999, Nelson Mandela was the President of *South Africa/Zimbabwe.*

e The Spice Girls were popular *in the 1990s/in the 1970s.*

f Marie Curie was born in *Warsaw/Paris.*

g John Lennon and Paul McCartney (members of The Beatles) were both originally from *London/Liverpool.*

h Marilyn Monroe's real name was *Norma Jean Baker/Jean Harlow.*

b) 📼 [7.1] Listen and check.

Grammar

Past Simple: *was* and *were*
Complete the gaps.

➕	➖	❓
I was.	I wasn't	.... I?
he/she/it	he/she/it	.... he/she/it?
you/we/they	you/we/they	.... you/we/they?

▶ *Language summary A page 145.*

Practice

1 Write sentences about five of the famous people in the pictures.

a   Picasso wasn't French, he was Spanish.

2 Make true sentences with *was*, *wasn't*, *were* or *weren't*.

a   I *was/wasn't* born in the 1980s.
b   I *was/wasn't* at home at ten o'clock last night.
c   The weather *was/wasn't* very good yesterday.
d   The 1990s *were/weren't* a good time for my country.
e   I *was/wasn't* late for class today.
f   My first teacher *was/wasn't* a woman.

3 **a)** Complete the questions with *was* or *were*.

1   Where ...were.... you born? Where .... your parents born?
2   Where .... you at eight o'clock last night?
3   When .... your last birthday? How old .... you?
4   What programmes .... on television last night?
5   .... anybody late for class today? Who?

b) Match answers a–e with questions 1–5.

a   It was in June – I was twenty-one! **Question 3**
b   I don't know – I think there was a film, or maybe a football match …
c   Yes, Patrick was late – as usual!
d   I was born in London. My father and mother were born in Ireland.
e   I was at home with my family.

c) 🔊 [7.2] Now listen and check your answers.

4 Ask and answer questions 1–5 from Exercise 3 in pairs. Tell the class about your partner.

> Jan was born in Prague. His parents were born in Bruno.

> At eight o'clock last night Nil was at her friend's house.

Pronunciation

1 🔊 [7.3] Listen and complete the gaps with present or past forms of *be*.
a   Where ...are.... the children?
b   Where .... you?
c   The train .... fast.
d   The food .... very good.
e   You .... here yesterday.
f   They .... on holiday.
g   They .... at home.
h   We .... at school.

2 Listen again and practise.

Reading

Ordinary lives, important ideas

1 Tim Berners-Lee invented something very important. Do you know what it was?

2 [MD] Check the meaning of the words in the box.

> ordinary   surprising   become   interested in
> graduate   a network   decide   linked

3 Read the text. Then complete the fact file.

Tim Berners-Lee looks ordinary – he is about 45 years old and has brown hair. His life is quite normal – he was born in England, but his home is now in Massachusetts, USA. But, in 1989, Tim had a very important idea. He invented the World Wide Web (www!)

Tim went to school in London. His parents both worked with computers, so it isn't surprising that he loved computers from an early age. When he was eighteen, he left school and went to Oxford University, where he studied Physics. At Oxford, he became more and more interested in computers, and he made his first computer from an old television. He graduated in 1976 and got a job with a computer company in Dorset, England. In 1989, he went to work in Switzerland, where he first had the idea of an international information network linked by computer … and he decided to call it the World Wide Web. In 1994, he went to live in the United States, where he now works. In 1995, he wrote an article in *The New York Times* where he said 'The Web is a Universe of information: it is for everyone.' His idea of a web, where people from all over the world can exchange information, is now real.

Tim Berners-Lee: Fact file	
His important idea	
Place of birth	
Place(s) of study	
Place(s) of work	
Personal details	
Now lives in	

Language focus 2

Past Simple: regular and irregular verbs

1 a) Look back at the text about Tim Berners-Lee. Find **two** sentences about his life now, and **two** sentences about his life in the past.

b) [MD] Underline the verbs in the sentences and say if they are regular or irregular. Check your answer in the mini-dictionary.

Grammar

1 Regular verbs:
a Find the past forms in the text.

invent .invented..

work ....

love ....

study ....

graduate ....

decide ....

b How do we form the Past Simple of **regular** verbs?

2 Irregular verbs
Find the past forms in the text.

have ....

go ....

leave ....

become ....

make ....

get ....

write ....

▶ *Language summary B page 145.*

Practice

1 [MD] Check the meaning of the words in the box. Then read the text and put the verbs into the past tense.

> childhood   a farm   zoology   a poem   the environment

Rachel Carson; mother of the environmental movement

The Story of Rachel Carson

Rachel (a) ..ᴡᴀѕ.. (*be*) born in a small town in Pennsylvania, U.S.A. – in 1907. She (b) .... (*have*) a happy childhood with her family on a small farm. She soon (c) .... (*become*) very interested in nature, and (d) .... (*write*) poems about her favourite animals. At the age of 18, she (e) .... (*leave*) her home town and (f) .... (*go*) to study zoology at the Pennsylvania College for Women.

2 [MD] Put these regular verbs in the past to complete the story.

> work   die   help   love   study   believe

Rachel (a) .ɢʀᴀᴅᴜᴀᴛᴇᴅ. from the Pennsylvania College for Women in 1929; she then (b) .... at John Hopkins University in Baltimore. For many years she (c) .... for the US government as a biologist. Rachel always (d) .... nature, and (e) .... that people, animals and plants are all linked. Her books (f) .... people to understand the importance of the environment for everyone. Now people call her 'The Mother of the Environmental Movement'. She (g) .... in 1964, aged fifty-seven.

Pronunciation

1 [🔊] [7.4] Listen and mark the number of syllables and the stress. Practise saying the verbs.

```
  •           • •          •   • •
worked    studied    invented

helped    finished    decided

believed    graduated

travelled    started    loved

walked    wanted
```

3 [MD] Here is some more information about the famous people on page 56. Find the past form of new verbs in your mini-dictionary.

Nelson Mandela (a) .... (*spend*) twenty-seven years in prison. Before that, he (b) .... (*be*) a lawyer.

Abba (c) .... (*write*) most of their songs in English. They (d) .... (*sell*) millions of records in the 70s and 80s.

John Lennon and Paul McCartney first (e) .... (*meet*) at a party when they (f) .... (*be*) students.

Marilyn Monroe (g) .... (*change*) her name before she (h) .... (*become*) famous.

Marie Curie and her husband Pierre Curie (i) .... (*discover*) radium. She (j) .... (*win*) the Nobel Prize twice, in 1903 and again in 1911.

Pablo Picasso (k) .... (*leave*) Spain in 1904. He (l) .... (*live*) in France for most of his life. He (m) .... (*die*) in 1973.

Listening
My great-grandfather

George Zawiló

Tessa (right) with her sister
and great-grandparents

1 [7.5] Listen to Tessa talking about her great-grandfather, George. Answer these questions.

a Where was George born?
b Where did he live before the war?
c Where did he live after the war?
d What nationality was his wife?

2 a) Put the verb into the past form then match the two parts of the sentences.

1 Tessa only (*know*) knew
2 George (*die*)
3 George (*be*) born
4 The Second World War (*begin*)
5 When the soldiers (*come*)
6 He (*walk*)
7 It (*take*) him
8 When the war (*end*)
9 He (*meet*) her great-grandmother

a he (*decide*) to leave Poland.
b about three months.
c her great-grandfather George for a few years.
d he (*go*) to live in England.
e in the 1920s.
f and they (*get*) married.
g when Tessa (*be*) about ten.
h in 1939.
i from Poland to Egypt.

b) [7.5] Now listen and check your answers.

3 What do you know about your grandparents', or great-grandparents' lives? Tell your partner:

• their names.
• where they were originally from.
• when they were born.
• when and where they met/ got married.
• any other interesting information.

60

Elvis Presley

Wilhelm Roentgen

Mozart as a child

Vocabulary

Past time phrases

1 a) 🔊 [7.6] Listen and say these years.

1995	1933	1968	1914	1905
1848	1779	1333	1709	2002

b) Write down five more years. Your partner says them.

2 📼 Complete the sentences with a time phrase from the box.

in the 1950s	in the sixteenth century	when he was eight
~~in 1895~~	about 30 years ago	

a The German scientist Wilhelm Roentgen discovered X-rays ..in..
  1895.
b The Austrian composer Wolfgang Amadeus Mozart wrote his first
  symphony ....
c Rock 'n' roll first became popular ....
d The Sony electronics company made the first video cassette
  recorder ....
e William Shakespeare wrote *Romeo and Juliet* ....

3 a) Put the verbs in the past tense, then use a time phrase to
  complete the sentences.

1 My mother (*be*) born in ....
2 My father (*be*) born in ....
3 I (*go*) to primary school from .... to ....
4 I (*learn*) to walk when ....
5 I (*start*) learning English .... ago.
6 My last holiday (*be*) .... ago.
7 My great-grandparents (*be*) born ....
8 I (*have*) breakfast .... ago.
9 I first (*meet*) my English teacher .... ago.
10 I (*move*) to my present address in ....

b) Compare your answers in pairs.

▶ *Language summary C page 145.*

Tell a life story

Preparation for task

1 Marlene is a singer. She comes from Swansea, a town in Wales. What can you see in each picture.

2 [7.7] Listen to Marlene talking about the pictures. Which picture does she describe in each extract?

Extract A = picture ☐
Extract B = picture ☐
Extract C = picture ☐
Extract D = picture ☐
Extract E = picture ☐
Extract F = picture ☐

Task

1 Draw six simple pictures for different times in your life. Think about what to say for each picture.

2 Talk to a partner about your pictures.

▶ *Useful language.*

3 Choose three interesting things to tell the class about your partner.

Real life

Ordinal numbers, dates and years

1 [7.8] Match the dates a–g with the ordinal numbers in the box. Listen and practise saying the dates.

third   twelfth   ~~first~~   thirtieth   second   twentieth   fifth

▶ *Language summary D page 145.*

2 [7.9] Circle the numbers you hear.

a	1	1st		e	13	30th		i	1798	1789
b	2	2nd		f	11	11th		j	1918	1980
c	24	24th		g	23	23rd		k	1990	1999
d	20th	21st		h	1500	1600				

3 Practise saying other dates and numbers that you **didn't** hear.

4 **a)** What do you know about George Washington and Christopher Columbus?

b) Work in pairs to find information about Washington and Columbus. **Student A** look at page 136. **Student B** look at page 139. Complete the missing information.

George Washington

Christopher Columbus

Do you remember?

1 **Complete the gaps with** *was, wasn't, were* **or** *weren't.*

In Module 1,

a)   there ..*were*.. two Japanese people.

b)   there .... a student card. It .... James Burden's.

c)   there .... some pictures of sportsmen and women.

In Module 2,

d)   there .... some water.

e)   there .... any dogs.

In Module 3,

f)   there .... some coke.

g)   there .... a postcard of a shopping centre.

h)   the time in London .... three o'clock.

In Module 4,

i)   there .... any Spanish food.

j)   there .... a spider.

In Module 5,

k)   there .... four different ways to go to Heathrow airport.

l)   there .... some pictures of women.

In Module 6,

m)   there .... any pasta.

n)   there .... some jokes.

2 **Write the missing letters to make the present and past forms of the verbs.**

PRESENT	PAST
c o̲ m e	c a̲ m e
m a _ e	m a _ e
w r _ t e	w r _ t e
b e c _ m e	b e c _ m e
k n _ w	k n _ w
g _ t	g _ t
m _ _ t	m _ t
t _ k _	t _ _ k

3 **a) Match the two parts of the sentences.**

1) I went   a) with a law firm
2) I left   b) computers
3) I worked with   c) three children
4) I became interested   d) school
5) I got   e) in languages
6) I got a job   f) married
7) I had   g) to university

b) Now test your partner.

I went ...?   ... to university

4 **Put a word from the box in the correct place in the sentences.**

> from   in   ago   ~~when~~   in   was   ago   in

a)   I went to Turkey ⟍ I was seventeen.
         when

b)   The artist Leonardo da Vinci lived the fifteenth century.

c)   The lesson finished half an hour.

d)   My uncle started riding a motorbike when he thirteen.

e)   *The Simpsons* was a popular television show the 1990s.

f)   Chris first met Sally about two months.

g)   Angela worked as an engineer 1992 to 1998.

h)   Vladimir Putin became President of Russia 2000.

Fact or fiction?

> ▶ **Past Simple:** negative
> ▶ **Past Simple:** questions
> ▶ **Vocabulary:** common verbs in the Past Simple
>
> **Task:** *Do It Yourself* story

Vocabulary

Common verbs in the Past Simple

1 [MD] Check the meaning of verbs a–m and write the past tense.

a   buy ...**bought**...

b   drink ....

c   drive ....

d   eat ....

e   fall ....

f   find ....

g   give ....

h   read ....

i   see ....

j   sleep ....

k   wake up ....

l   wear ....

m   write ....

2 **a)** Match sentences a–f with pictures 1–6. Complete the gaps with a verb from Exercise 1 in the Past Simple.

a   A man and two children ☑ ...**slept**... in a tree and when they .... they .... some dinosaurs.

b   Two young women .... a car for $100 and .... across the United States from east to west. ☐

c   A little girl .... a bottle with the words 'DRINK ME': she .... it and suddenly she was three metres tall! ☐

d   An old woman .... an apple to a young woman: she .... it and .... asleep for a long time. ☐

e   After her husband died, the Queen always .... black. ☐

f   A girl .... a diary that people .... after she died. ☐

b) Do you know which films the pictures come from?

Tarzan lived in the African jungle. He rode a motorbike. One day he met Jane, a beautiful girl, and they fell in love.

Pronunciation

1 🔲 [8.1] Look at the past forms of the verbs, and listen to the pronunciation. Is the sound underlined the same (S) or different (D)?

a w<u>ore</u>   b<u>ough</u>t   S
b w<u>o</u>ke up   dr<u>o</u>ve
c g<u>a</u>ve   dr<u>a</u>nk
d f<u>e</u>ll   r<u>ea</u>d
e sl<u>e</u>pt   <u>a</u>te

2 Listen again and practise saying the verbs.

Language focus 1

Past Simple: negative

1 **a)** Look at the pictures. What do you know about the famous fictional characters?

b) 🔲 Read the information about the three characters in the pictures. <u>Underline</u> the information which **isn't** true.

2 **a)** 🔲 [8.2] Listen to the correct answers.

b) 🔲 [8.3] Listen and complete the gaps.

1 Robin Hood .<u>didn't</u>.<u>give</u>. his money to Maid Marian. He .... it to poor people.

2 Dracula .... in a castle in Brazil. He .... in Transylvania.

Robin Hood lived in a forest in England. He and his friends always wore green clothes. He took money from rich people, and gave it to his girlfriend, Maid Marian.

Grammar

Past Simple: negative
We make the negative form with:
didn't + verb
*He **didn't live** in Brazil.*
(didn't = did not)

▶ *Language summary A page 145.*

Dracula was a vampire who lived in a castle in Brazil. He always slept during the day, but at night he became a bat and drank human blood.

Practice

1 **a)** 🔲 The picture is a scene from the story of *Romeo and Juliet* which takes place in Italy about 500 years ago. There are **eight** mistakes in the picture. Can you find them?

b) Make sentences using these verbs.

> wear   ride   use   have   eat   read

People didn't wear roller blades 500 years ago.

2 **a)** Put the verb in the correct form to make the sentence true for you. Compare your answers with a partner.

a   I (*go*) shopping last weekend.

> *I went shopping last weekend.*
> *I didn't go shopping last weekend.*

b   I (*have*) a coffee before this lesson.

c   I (*come*) to school by bus today.

d   I (*read*) in bed last night.

e   I (*have*) breakfast this morning.

f   I (*go*) out last Saturday night.

g   I (*have*) fish for dinner last night.

h   I (*sleep*) well last night.

b) Compare your answers with a partner.

I didn't have a coffee before the lesson.

I had a coffee, and some chocolate!

I came to school by bus today.

Me too!

Language focus 2

Past Simple: questions

1 **a)** Find these things in the four pictures: a *dragon*, a *prince*, and a *cave*.

b) 🔲 [8.4] Maggie is a tour guide. She's describing a legend to some tourists. Listen to her story and put the pictures in order 1–4.

2 Listen again. Write down the little boy's questions next to Maggie's answers.

a .... ? No, he didn't. He lived in a cave.

b .... ? No, he didn't. Only girls.

c .... ? Er … I don't know.

d .... ? Yes, he did.

Grammar

Past Simple: questions

🔲 [8.5] Complete the gaps.

.... *the dragon* .... *in this house?*

No, he .... *in a cave.*

.... *the dragon* .... *boys?*

We make the question form with:

did + subject + verb

Notice the short answers:

Yes, he **did**.

No, he **didn't**.

▶ **Language summary B/C page 145/146.**

Practice

1 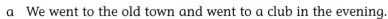 **a)** Remember when you were ten years old. Put a tick (✓) next to the things you **did** and a cross (✗) next to the things you **didn't do**.

a play football
b go abroad for your holidays
c wear jeans
d go out every Saturday night
e watch television in your room
f ride a bicycle
g play computer games
h have a mobile phone
i read the newspaper
j drink coffee

b) Ask your partner about these things.

When you were ten years old ... did you play football?

Yes, I did.

I don't remember.

c) Tell the class about you and your partner.

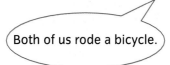

Both of us rode a bicycle.

2 Anna is asking Helena about her weekend. Complete questions 1–7 and match them with answers a–g.

1 Where ...did you... go?
2 Who/go with?
3 How/get there?
4 Why/go there?
5 What/think of it?
6 What/do there?
7 When/come back?

a We went to the old town and went to a club in the evening.
b By plane.
c We went to Prague.
d Early this morning!
e It was fantastic!
f Because someone told us about it.
g With my friend.

3 Ask your partner questions 1–7 about where he/she went:

a last weekend.
b last month.
c last year.
d when he/she was young.

4 Now write sentences about your partner.

Alain went to Madrid last month for a holiday.
He went with his family.
He went there by car.
They went because they like cities.
They visited the old town and went to a concert.
They came back three weeks ago.
They loved Madrid!

Listening

Interview with a writer of a very short story

1 　🔲 [8.6] Tina Ross won a competition to write a sixty word story for *Bellissima* magazine. Listen to an interview with Tina and write her answers to questions a–f.

a　What's the title of your very short story?

b　How long did it take you to write it?

c　Who are your favourite writers?

d　Where did you get the idea for the story?

e　What's the story about?

f　Did you expect to win the competition?

2 **a)** Here is Tina's short story. Put the sentences in the right order.

☐　On the last day, Charlie died.

☐　The next day he won ten million pounds.

☐　The government took all his money, but everyone in the street always remembered the incredible street party.

☑　Charlie bought a lottery ticket with a one pound coin: his last.

☐　Charlie gave a party for his neighbours – it lasted two weeks.

☐　But they couldn't remember who gave it.

b) 🔲 [8.7] Listen and check the order. Do you like the story?

Do it yourself story

Preparation for task

Match a word or phrase from the box to one of the pictures on the right. (There is more than one possible answer.)

> 'I've got a problem.'　a beautiful day
> 'Hello?'　woke up　looked out of the window
> telephone rang　got in his car and drove to …
> Suddenly, René saw　looked at his watch
> had breakfast

Task

1 Use the pictures to invent a story. Complete the gaps!

René woke up as usual at (a) ....
(When?) He looked out of the window.
It was another beautiful day in (b) ....
(Where?) He went downstairs and had his usual
breakfast: (c) .... and .... (What?) Before
he finished his meal, the phone rang. He answered
it. 'Hello?' Silence. Then … 'René?' A woman's
voice: he knew it immediately. It was (d) ....
(Who?) 'Yes.' he answered. 'Thank goodness it's
you, René. I've got a problem, and I need your
help. Meet me in one hour.'
René left the apartment, got in his car and drove to
(e) .... (Where?) He arrived at (f) ....
(What time?). She wasn't there. René looked at his
watch. Suddenly René saw (g) .... (Who?)
There was one important question in René's mind:
(h) '.............?' he asked. (i) ' ....' he/she
answered. (What did René do next?) (j) ....
(How did the story end?) (k) ....

2 **a)** Work in pairs. Ask questions to find out about your partner's story.

▶ *Useful language a) and b)*

b) How many differences are there between the two stories? Make a list.

In my story, René lived in New York, but in Joan's story he lived in Paris.

3 🔲 [8.8] Listen to the original story.

①

②

③

④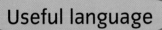

⑤

⑥

⑦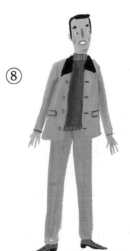

⑧

Useful language

a Asking questions

"When did she arrive?"

"Where did he go?"

"What did he do?"

"Why was he late?"

"What time did he arrive?"

"Who did he see?"

"How did the story end?"

b Talking about differences

"In my story, René didn't …"

"In my partner's story, …"

Real life: writing

Keep a diary in English

Martina is learning English. To practise, she writes a diary in English every day.

1 What do you think Martina writes in her English diary? Read and check.

Monday 23rd June

This morning I had an Economics exam - it wasn't very difficult.
After the exam I met Alex in the park. We had a coffee in the Metro Bar. I came home and studied for my exam tomorrow - French!!!

Tuesday 24th June

The French exam was horrible! I didn't finish and I felt very unhappy. I met Alex again and he walked home with me. We talked about our exams. He's really nice! He asked me to go to the cinema with him tomorrow night. Yes!!!

Wednesday 25th June

Alex and I went to see the new Brad Pitt film. I thought it was okay, but not fantastic - Alex thought it was rubbish! After the film we went to a club and had a fantastic time dancing ... etc!!! Alex brought me home at about 1.30, but it was awful because Mum and Dad were...

---

2 **MD** Check these words then answer the questions.

> an exam   horrible   awful   rubbish

a How old is Martina, do you think?

b What's her job?

c Were Monday, Tuesday and Wednesday good or bad days for her? Why?

d What was the end of the last sentence, do you think?

3 Write a diary in English for a week. If you can, buy a special notebook. After a week tell the other students about it.

Do you remember?

1 Match a verb with a word or phrase.

1	go	a	late
2	wear	b	a competition
3	give a present	c	a horse
4	wake up	d	to a friend
5	fall	e	abroad
6	win	f	a diary
7	ride	g	glasses
8	read	h	asleep

2 Find the past form of the verb and then write the base form.

swa saw see.   lefl ....
vedro ....   grobuth ....
stelp ....   pu weko ....
tens ....   erow ....
woter ....   tae ....
nufod ....   aveg ....

3 Tick (✓) the three correct sentences and correct the mistakes in the other four.

a How much sugar did you buy? ✓

b Did you find your money?

c She didn't lived in Ireland.

d Did they went to Russia?

e Steve didn't like the film.

f Did you slept well?

g I didn't had breakfast this morning.

4 Write questions about the underlined information.

.... I went to (a) New Zealand last month (b) with Jeff. We went there (c) because we wanted to visit my sister – she lives in Christchurch. We went (d) by plane from Sydney to Wellington and then we drove down to Christchurch. We had a really fantastic time! (e) We visited the mountains, we went horse-riding, and did lots of shopping! It was my first visit to New Zealand and (f) I loved it! We came back to Australia (g) two days ago ...

a Where did you go?

b Who .....

module 9

Buying and selling

▶ Comparative adjectives
▶ Superlative adjectives
▶ Vocabulary: shops and shopping

Task: choose souvenirs from your country

Language focus 1

Comparative adjectives

1 **a)** What do you know about cars? Think of:

- a **fast** car   a Ferrari
- an **expensive** car
- a **small** car
- a very **comfortable** car
- a very **ugly** car
- an **old** car
- an **easy** car to park

b) Look at the adjectives in **bold**. Match them with their opposites in the box.

fast   –   slow

cheap   uncomfortable
difficult   new   slow
attractive   big

2 Read about Juliana.

a What does Juliana want to buy? Why?

b How much does she want to spend?

FOR SALE
Green 1989 Magellen Micro
£325
Phone 5438799

FOR SALE
1985 Victa Deluxe – red,
very good condition
£650
Phone 5664635
evenings only

Juliana is a student. She wants to buy an old car to drive to university with her four friends. She wants to spend about £500, but she doesn't know much about cars. She sees these two advertisements.

3 **a)** Look at the advertisements and the pictures. Which of the two cars is: older? bigger? more expensive?

b) Look at the pictures. Which of these sentences do you think are true? Correct the sentences you think are wrong.

1 The Deluxe is faster than the Micro.
2 The Micro is more comfortable than the Deluxe.
3 The Deluxe is easier to park than the Micro.
4 The Micro is more expensive to run than the Deluxe.
5 The Micro is better for Juliana than the Deluxe.

I think the Deluxe is slower than the Micro.

Vocabulary

Shops and shopping

1 Match the pictures to one of the shops in the box.

> a clothes shop   a supermarket   a street market
> a pharmacy   a butcher's   a bookshop
> a newsagent's   a greengrocer's   a baker's
> a post office

2 Work with a partner. Ask and answer questions about shops a–j.

> Where is the nearest bookshop?

> It's in King Street.

3 a) Where do people normally buy these things in your country?

> a newspaper   potatoes   a dictionary
> toothpaste   bread   a pair of jeans   aspirin
> cigarettes   cakes   flowers   fruit   stamps

> You can buy a newspaper from a newsagent's, and sometimes from a bookshop.

b) Make a list of two other things you can buy in each shop.

Reading and writing

1 a) **MD** Check the meaning of the words in the box.

> jewellery   a carpet   a bird   a herb
> tropical fruit   natural medicine

b) Look at the pictures of different markets opposite. Which of them do you think is:

- the most exciting?
- the most lively?
- the most similar to markets in your country?
- the most colourful?
- the oldest?
- the most unusual?

Street Markets
Around the World

Do you want to buy a new pair of sunglasses? The latest CD? Or something for your dinner this evening? Nowadays, you can shop by telephone, by post or through your home computer: but for many people, the most exciting way to shop is also the most traditional – at a street market. You can find markets anywhere in the world. Here are five of them …

Every weekend, thousands of young people from all over London travel to Camden Market in an attractive area in the north of the city – it's the place to go for street fashion, jewellery, CDs and tapes … but many people just go for the lively atmosphere!

There are many 'floating markets' in Asia; perhaps the most famous is in Thailand, at a place called Damnoen Saduak, 100km from the capital city, Bangkok. From six in the morning to midday, every day, people sell fresh tropical fruit and vegetables from their boats.

The Grand Bazaar in Istanbul, Turkey, is more than 500 years old and it has more than four thousand shops under one roof! You can buy almost anything, but the most popular items for tourists are the beautiful rugs and carpets. It's open all day every day!

Many Belgians say that the Grand Place – in the centre of the capital city, Brussels, is the most beautiful square in the world. It is the home of a colourful flower market – open every day except Monday. On Monday, instead of flowers, there's a wonderful bird market!

One of the world's most unusual markets is in Mexico City: at the Sonora Market. As well as toys and birds, you can buy herbs and natural medicines which (they say) can help with anything – from problems at work to problems with your marriage! It's open every day from early in the morning till late at night.

2 Read the text about five different markets around the world.

a What are the names of the five markets?

b Where are the markets?

c What can you buy at each different market?

d When is each market open?

3 Write a short paragraph about a market you know.

The market is called … It's in …
It's open from …
It sells a lot of … and …
I often go there
I like it because …

Choose souvenirs from your country

Preparation for task

1 **a)** Match the words in the box with the pictures.

> tartan scarf   CD   pasta   doll   wine   book

b) Which country do you think these souvenirs come from?

2 🔲 [9.2] Listen to some people talking about one of the souvenirs in the picture. Complete the sentences below.

CARLA: The (a) .... food in the world comes from Italy – so it's a good idea to buy some (b) ....

HELENA: My country is very (c) .... for music – especially samba music. I think a CD of typical samba music from Brazil is a very good (d) ....

GREG: If you like (e) ...., you can buy a book by a Polish writer, her name is Wisława Szymborska.

GUY: A good thing (f) .... is a bottle of wine, French wine (g) .... all around the world ... and the best wine comes from Bordeaux, in southwest France ...

3 Read the details about the people below.

Mark and Ellen want to buy some typical souvenirs from your country to take back to the United States.

Tom wants to buy a souvenir for his two children, (a boy aged five and a girl aged eight) and something for his wife – she likes clothes.

Jane is very interested in food and drink. She wants to buy some typical food and drink to take home with her.

Helen loves music and reading ... she especially likes folk music and literature.

Task

1 Work individually. Write down a souvenir from your town or country for three of the people.

- Mark and Ellen
- Tom
- Jane
- Helen

2 Work in groups of three or four. Decide the best souvenir for each of the people in the pictures.

▶ *See Useful language a) and b)*

3 Tell the rest of the group what you decided. How many people chose the same things as souvenirs?

▶ *See Useful language c)*

Real life

Asking in shops

1 **a)** Look at pictures a–f. What kind of shops are they?

b) 🔊 [9.3] Listen to six short conversations Which conversation goes with each picture?

Recording 1 = picture d

2

a) Match questions 1–6 with answers a–f.

1 Do you sell toothpaste?
2 Do you accept credit cards?
3 Have you got this in a smaller size?
4 How much is this?
5 What time do you close?
6 Can I have one of those, please?

a This one?
b It's £25.
c At eight o'clock.
d Let me check for you.
e Yes, Visa or Mastercard.
f No, we don't. Try the pharmacy.

b) 🔊 [9.3] Listen again and check your answers.

3

a) Peter is on holiday. Look at his shopping list.

postcards for home ✔
baseball cap
stamps
fruit
batteries for camera
bread and cake
sunglasses
toothpaste

b) 🔊 [9.4] Listen to Peter's conversations in different shops. Tick (✓) the things he bought.

c) Look at the tapescripts on page 156 and practise the conversations.

4

Practise two conversations with a customer and shop assistant in a general store.

Student A: Look at page 136.
Student B: Look at page 137.

80

Do you remember?

1

a) Write three adjectives to describe:

a your teacher.
   tall, nice, easy to understand
b your classroom.
c the school.
d your city or town.
e your favourite sport.

b) Read out your adjectives and guess the subject.

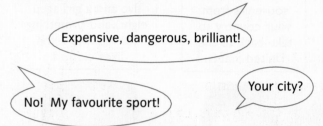

Expensive, dangerous, brilliant!

No! My favourite sport!

Your city?

2

a) Complete the gaps with the comparative or superlative form .

1 Who's ...taller... *(tall)*, you or your teacher?
2 What's .... *(expensive)* thing you have in your house?
3 Which is .... *(good)* – watching a video at home or going to the cinema?
4 What is/was .... *(difficult)* subject at school for you?
5 Which is.................. *(easy)* for you – speaking or understanding English?
6 What's .... *(comfortable)* – travelling by car, by train or by plane?
7 Which is .... *(nice)* – a day in the city or a day in the country?

b) Work with a partner and ask and answer questions 1–7.

3 Write three adjectives under each stress pattern.

• • •   • •   • • •
difficult friendly expensive

popular   modern   fantastic   common
interesting   successful   expensive

module 10

Street life

▶ **Vocabulary**: describing people; clothes
▶ **Present Continuous**
▶ **Present Simple and Present Continuous**

Task: describe and draw a picture

Vocabulary 1

Describing people

1 **a)** Work in pairs. Look at the pictures of four people in the street. Who:

1 has got a moustache?
 Paolo and Mike

2 has got a beard?

3 is black?

4 has got a ponytail?

5 is in her thirties?

6 is very tall and slim?

7 has got blue eyes?

8 has got short hair?

9 has got long hair?

10 is very good-looking?

11 wears glasses?

12 wears an earring?

13 has got a shaved head?

14 has got medium-length hair?

15 has got blonde hair?

16 has got dark hair?

b) Use the sentences above to describe the people in the pictures.

Kamilla

Paolo

Sheena

Mike

2 **a)** Choose someone in your class. Write **five** sentences about him or her, like this:

She's got long hair.
She's in her twenties.
She's tall.

She's got blue eyes.
She doesn't wear glasses.
WHO IS SHE?

b) Give your sentences to another pair. Can they guess who it is?

Vocabulary 2

Clothes

1 Match the words in the box with pictures a–n.

> shoes   shirt   trousers   tights   pullover
> top   trainers   jeans   earrings   tie
> suit   skirt   jacket   coat

2 Who usually wears these clothes – men, women or both?

tights – women

3 a) Work with a partner. Complete the questions about people in your class.

1 Who is wearing *black jeans*?
2 Who is wearing ....?
3 How many people are wearing ....?
4 What colour are ....'s shoes?
5 What colour is ....'s ....?
6 Is .... wearing earrings?
7 Is .... wearing ....?

b) Work with a new partner. Ask and answer the questions. Don't look!

Who is wearing black jeans?

Irena!

Listening

Andy

Michelle

1 The people in the pictures wear a uniform in their jobs. What are their jobs?

2 🎧 [10.2] Listen to Andy and Michelle talking about their uniforms and answer the questions.

a Which clothes do they talk about?
b What adjectives do they use to describe their uniforms?
c Do they like their uniforms?

3 Do you wear a uniform at school or at work? Which uniforms in your country do you like?

Language focus 2

Present Simple and Present Continuous

It's Friday night and Michelle is getting ready
to go out. At work, Michelle wears dark
colours and very little make-up, so when
she goes out she wears bright colours.
This evening she's wearing a new pink top,
a blue skirt and quite a lot of make-up!

a) In what ways does Michelle look different
from the photo on page 84?

b) [MD] Read about Michelle and answer the
questions.

a What's Michelle doing at the moment?

b What's she wearing?

c What kind of colours does she wear at work?

d What colours does she wear to go out?

e Does she wear a lot of make-up at work?

f Is she wearing make-up tonight?

Grammar

1 (Circle) the correct answers.

Present Simple:
*She **wears** dark colours at work.*
This is *usually true/happening now.*

Present Continuous:
*She**'s wearing** a pink dress tonight*
This is *usually true/happening now.*

2a Words we use with the Present Simple:
usually always often normally every day

b Words we use with the Present
Continuous:
now   today   at the moment

▶ *Language summary C page 146.*

Practice

Choose the best verb form, Present Simple or
Present Continuous.

'Right now I
(a) .... *(go)* for a
jog in the park,
that's why I (b) ....
(wear) shorts. I
(c) .... *(not wear)*
shorts usually.... I
(d) .... *(hate)*
shorts, and most of
all... I (e) ....'
(hate) my legs!'

'It's fantastic! It's only
March and it's really, really
hot – the sun (f) .... *(shine)*
and people (g) .... *(wear)*
tee-shirts! I (h) .... *(have)*
coffee outside, it's incredible!
Normally in this city it
(i) .... *(rain)* all the time in
March – and sometimes it
(j) .... *(snow)*, but today's
beautiful!'

Consolidation ──── modules 6–10

A Grammar: Present Simple, Present Continuous, Past Simple

Circle the correct form of the verb.

Hi Jeff,
I (1) *write/'m writing/wrote* this e-mail from sunny Rome where I (2) *sit/'m sitting/sat* on a balcony in the city centre and I've got some brilliant news! Last Saturday I (3) *get/'m getting/got* married!
My wife's name is Laura and she (4) *comes/'s coming/came* from Sicily. She's a photographer and she (5) *works/'s working/worked* for 'Amica', a famous Italian magazine. We (6) *meet/'re meeting/met* at a party in Milan about a month ago and one week later we (7) *decide/'re deciding/decided* to get married! We (8) *don't have/aren't having/didn't have* a big wedding – only her parents and a few Italian friends.
We (9) *come back/'re coming back/came back* to Rome two days ago and at the moment we (10) *stay/'re staying/stayed* in Laura's apartment because it's bigger than mine and nearer Laura's workplace.
Come and visit us! I'm sure you'll like Laura and she (11) *wants/'s wanting/wanted* to meet all my friends.
Our address is ....

B Reading and speaking: snacks around the world

1 Read about snacks in Germany, Brazil and Japan. Complete the gaps with *a/an*, *some*, *any* or *no*.

'Well I often have (1)....a.... a snack at about eleven in the morning. I usually go to a kiosk near here and buy (2).......... sausage, and then I eat it, standing up at a small table near the kiosk. Then at about four o'clock we usually stop work and have (3).......... cup of coffee and (4).......... cakes.'
Suzanne, Germany

'I don't usually have (5).......... food in the middle of the morning, but in the afternoon, at about five o'clock, I sometimes have a coffee. Yesterday, for example, I had (6).......... bread roll and (7).......... cheese. I get very hungry in the afternoons! Oh, yes, and I had (8).......... iced tea. You can buy it at the beach or on the streets – it's very popular in Brazil.'
Renato, Brazil

'In Japan we eat food from all over the world, and young people like European snacks. Older people like more traditional food. For example, every afternoon my grandfather has (9).......... Japanese sweets with traditional green tea. At work, on weekdays we usually have a 'three o'clock snack'. Today I had (10).......... biscuits and tea, but (11).......... milk! I find it very strange that English people have milk in their tea!'
Mariko, Japan

2 Work with a partner. Ask and answer these questions:

a Do you have snacks between meals?
b What did you have yesterday?

C Speaking: real life

1 What do you say in the following situations?

a You are in a restaurant and you want to pay. What do you say to the waiter?
b You are in a street market. You want to buy a tee-shirt. Ask about the price.
c You are phoning a pizza service. You want two large pizzas. What do you say?
d You are buying a ticket in a railway station. The clerk says the price of the ticket but you don't understand him. What do you say?
e You are in a shop. You want to buy some shampoo but you can't see any. What do you ask the shop assistant?
f You are in a shop and you want to buy a tee-shirt, but it's too small for you. What do you ask the shop assistant?
g You are in a shop. An assistant asks you 'Can I help you?' but you don't want to buy anything at the moment. What do you say?

2 🔊 [1] Listen and check. Are your questions the same?

3 Practise the situations in pairs.

D Reading and speaking: comparatives and superlatives

1 Read this about four holidays. Which country is each holiday in? Where can you:

a   see a lot of animals? b   go to the beach?

c   go skiing? d   visit a historic town?

Come to Courchevel!

Courchevel, in the French Alps, has the largest ski area in the world with 250 lifts and 600 km of perfect snow. The night life is very active, there are bars and clubs open till late, and fantastic restaurants for all tastes.
The Hotel D'Armor is a modern building with 350 rooms, a swimming pool and sauna, and it's only five minutes from the nearest ski lift.
Prices from £699.00 a week, including ski pass and ski hire.

www.D'Armor.uk.com.

Ölüdeniz

Situated in beautiful Ölüdeniz, we are only five minutes from the sea. Our very modern Turkish apartment sleeps five and has its own small garden. The town of Fethiye, with its old streets and buildings, is only fifteen km away. If you want a quiet, peaceful break near the sea, then this is perfect for you!

£650 a week

hotels.wec-net.com.

Pelion Peninsula

One and two bedroom traditional apartments near the small but cosmopolitan town of Agios Ioannis on the Pelion peninsula. Enjoy the sun and the wonderful Greek food!
The apartments are self-catering and are only thirty minutes, walk from the beautiful Papa Nero beach.
Only **£450 a week** for a two bedroom apartment.

www.heliostravel.co.uk

African Adventure!

Kenya – Tanzania – Namibia – Botswana – South Africa – Uganda – Zambia and Malawi. We are simply the best for safaris. Small groups, friendly guides. Come canoeing, riding, and camping! See elephants, lions and other animals in the wild!
Tours are three, five or six weeks.
Prices from £1,350 for three weeks.

Tel 020 7482 142

www.africanadven.co.uk

2 Which is the best holiday for these people?

| expensive | cheap | quiet | busy | exciting |
| good | long | old | near | easy |

a   Adriana (22) and Sueli (23) are from Mexico. They like exciting holidays and want to meet other young people. They like dancing and sport. They want to go on holiday for two or three weeks, but they don't want to spend a lot of money.

b   Tanya and Rod Kilroy are from Canada. They've got two children, Jayne, aged 6, and Tom, aged 8, and they are looking for a quiet family holiday near the sea. They like old places. They haven't got a lot of money.

E Listening: song: *Return to Sender*

🔊 [2] Listen to the song and complete the gaps, then compare your answer with a partner.
Student A Turn to page 140. **Student B** Turn to page 133.

F Vocabulary

Find three words for each topic.

O	R	A	N	G	E	J	U	I	C	E	D
N	A	P	U	R	G	E	P	B	E	N	K
I	C	H	E	A	S	A	T	A	R	P	I
B	U	S	Y	D	W	N	O	K	E	O	O
O	P	U	N	U	T	S	Y	E	A	T	S
U	B	I	W	A	I	L	O	R	L	G	K
G	A	T	I	T	R	O	U	S	E	R	S
H	W	I	N	E	X	S	N	E	W	A	T
T	R	O	F	E	L	L	G	Z	I	P	Y
U	O	Y	A	R	D	E	C	I	D	E	O
N	T	A	B	U	T	C	H	E	R	S	U
B	E	L	I	E	V	E	W	B	E	E	R

a food   grapes

b drink

c clothes

d regular verbs

e past verbs

f adjectives

g shops

module 11

The world around us

► *Can* and *can't* for ability
► Question words

Task: do a general knowledge quiz

Language focus 1

Can and *can't* for ability

Read the facts below. Which did you already know?

Did you know ?

A cheetah can run at up to a hundred kilometres per hour.

A dog can't see colours.

A new baby can see shapes clearly from the moment he is born.

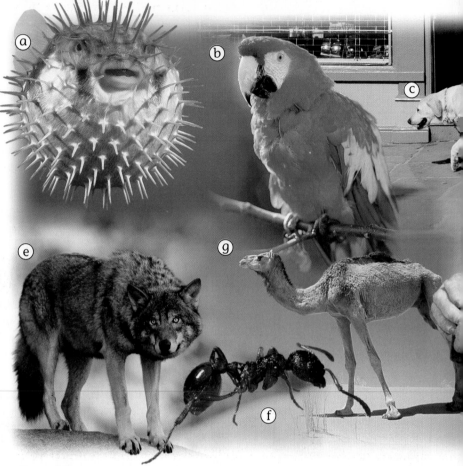

Grammar

Complete the gaps with can or can't.

➕ *A dog .... see black and white only.*

➖ *It .... see yellow, red or blue.*

❓ *............ a cheetah see colours?*

► **Language summary A page 147.**

Practice

1 🎧 Make sentences using words from the three columns.

A parrot can fly, but it can't paint pictures.

a parrot		fly
a chimpanzee		talk
a seven-year-old child		swim
	can	walk
a dolphin		paint pictures
	can't	read and write
a one-month-old baby		communicate
a one-month-old kitten		feed itself

2 If you are not sure, ask other students.

Can a chimpanzee swim?

I'm not sure.

I think so.

Reading

1 Discuss the following questions in small groups.

a Which of the animals in the pictures do you know? Where do they come from?

b Which animals attack or kill humans?

2 Read the text below. One of the statements is false, the others are all true. Which do you think is false? (Check your answer on page 136.)

3 Work with a partner. Which do you think is the most amazing fact?

Amazing animal facts!

The tuna is the world's fastest fish. It can swim at up to seventy-five kilometres per hour.

Camels can live up to twelve days without water.

Chimpanzees can't talk but they can learn sign language. Some chimps learn up to 240 signs.

The puffer fish, a small fish which lives in the Pacific Ocean, contains poison which can kill a human in just twenty minutes.

Guide dogs are colourblind, so they cannot see the difference between a green and a red light. They watch the traffic to see when it is safe to cross the road.

Koalas only eat one thing – the leaves of the eucalyptus tree. They don't even drink water!

Wolves attack and kill more than twenty people every year.

The Arctic tern, a bird which lives in North America and the Arctic, flies to the Antarctic and back every year – a journey of about forty thousand kilometres.

The blue whale is the world's largest animal – it weighs about a hundred and fifty tonnes.

There are at least ten thousand billion ants in the world, and only about six billion humans – that's 1,166 ants for every human!

Language focus 2
Question words

1 a) Work in pairs. Look at the quiz. How many questions can you answer **without** looking at page 91.

b) Look back and check your answers.

Animal Quiz

a (How fast) can a cheetah run?

b What kind of fish can kill you?

c How long can a camel live without water?

d Which colours can dogs see?

e How do guide dogs know when it is safe to cross the road?

f What do koalas eat?

g How far do Arctic terns fly every year?

h How much does a blue whale weigh?

i How many ants are there in the world?

2 (Circle) the question words or phrases.

Grammar

1 (Circle) the correct answer.

a We use **what** when there are **many/only a few** possible answers:
   What *does a koala drink?*

b We use **which** when there are **many/only a few** possible answers:
   Which *of these animals kill humans: wolves, spiders or whales?*

2 Do you remember? Complete the rule.
   We use *how many* with .... nouns.
   We use *how much* with .... nouns.

3 There are many other two-word questions with *how*, *what* and *which*. Match the question words to the answers.

a How long ...?   • a hundred kilometres per hour
b How often ...?   • New York
c How far ...?   • ten kilometres
d How fast ...?   • lions
e Which city ...?   • rock and pop
f Which animals ...?   • three hours
g What kind of music ...? • every day

▶ *Language summary B page 147.*

Practice

1 (Circle) the correct question words below. Use the answer to help you, where necessary.

a *Which/What* do whales eat?

b *How much/How many* water do people need to drink?

c *How much/How many* pets have you got?

d *What/Which* do you like best, cats or dogs?

e *What/Which* is your dog's name?

f *How long/How much* do sharks usually live?

g *How long/How often* do you need to feed a baby?
   (Every three or four hours, at least.)

h *How fast/How far* do most people walk?
   (About five to six kilometres an hour.)

i *How fast/How far* can you swim?
   (About five hundred metres.)

j *How much/How often* do you go swimming?
   (Two or three times a week.)

2 a) We use these different question words with different verb forms:

When <u>did</u> you <u>start</u> learning English?
Which other languages <u>do</u> you <u>speak</u>?
How far <u>can</u> you <u>swim</u>?

Make at least **six** questions using boxes A, B and C.

Ⓐ
When
What
What kind of music
Where
Which other languages
How
How often
How far
How fast
How many cousins
Which
How much money

Ⓑ
can you
do you
is
did you (last)
have you
were you

Ⓒ
get to school?
got?
like most?
your home from here?
born?
go to the cinema?
have for breakfast?
prefer, coffee or tea?
swim?
speak?
start learning English?

b) Spend a few minutes learning your questions. Ask three other students.

c) Tell the class something you learnt about each person.

Listening
Man's best friend?

1 Ask and answer these questions with a partner.

a   Do you have a pet dog or cat?
b   Would you like to have one? Why/Why not?
c   Do you have any other pets?

2 [MD] Look at activities a–g and check any new words. Which do you associate with dogs (D) and which do you associate with cats (C)?

a   having kittens   ☑C   e   finding drugs for customs officers   ☐
b   racing   ☐   f   hunting for mice and birds   ☐
c   helping the blind ☐   g   being very clean   ☐
d   being very lazy ☐

3 a) Questions 1–7 are all about cats. How many can you answer?

1   How many cats are there in the world today?
2   What do they eat?
3   How many hours a day do they sleep?
4   How long are female cats pregnant?
5   How many kittens do they have at one time?
6   How many kinds ('breeds') of cat are there?
7   What is special about sphynx cats?

b) [▭] [11.1] Now listen to the first part of a radio programme on cats and check your answers. Are any of them surprising?

4 🔊 [11.2] The second part of the programme is about dogs. Read the text below, then listen and complete the gaps.

People say that (1) a dog is a man's best friend . People and dogs first started living together about ten thousand years ago. Now there are (2)............... dogs just in the USA – the Americans spend over (3)............... on dog food every year – four times what they spend on baby food.

Altogether there are about (4)............... breeds of dog. Many dogs work for humans, doing jobs such as helping the blind, helping the police and customs officers to find drugs, and even racing!

Greyhound racing is popular (5)............................... . The fastest greyhounds can run as fast as (6)............................... kilometres per hour.

Perhaps the most famous working dog was Rin Tin Tin who died in (7)............... . He earned his money by (8)............... – he made (9)............... films and earned about $44,000 for each one!

5 Make questions about gaps 1–9. Then ask a partner.

When ...   What ...   Where ...
How ...   How much ...
How many ...(x3)   How fast ...

1 What do people say about dogs?

Do a general knowledge quiz

Preparation for task

1 **a)** 📖 Read the general knowledge quiz and complete the gaps. Check any new words in your mini-dictionary.

b) 🔊 [11.3] Listen to the questions and check your answers.

2 Now answer the questions in groups.

3 🔊 [11.4] Listen and check your answers. How many of the questions did you answer correctly?

1 .... language or languages do people speak in Canada?
A English   B French   C English and French

2 .... was the Hollywood actor Arnold Schwarzenegger born?
A Austria   B Germany   C the United States

3 .... players are there in a basketball team?
A five   B eight   C eleven

4 .... does it take to boil an egg?
A about 30 to 40 seconds   B about 3 to 4 minutes
C about 30 to 40 minutes

5 .... did Bill Clinton become President of the United States?
A 1990   B 1992   C 1996

6 .... is the biggest desert in the world?
A The Arabian Desert   B The Gobi Desert   C The Sahara Desert

7 .... did Joseph Niépce invent the first camera?
A 1726   B 1826   C 1926

8 .... is it from the Earth to the Moon?
A 38,000 km   B 380,000 km   C 3.8 million km

9 .... did France win the World Cup in football?
A in 1966 only   B in 1966 and 1998   C in 1998 only

10 Sushi is a popular type of food. .... does it come from?
A China   B India   C Japan

Useful language

a Asking questions:

"When did (*Bill Clinton*) become (*president*)?"

"Where was (*Marilyn Monroe*) born?"

"What language do people speak in (*Switzerland*)?"

"What's the capital of (*Canada*)?"

"How far is it from (*Paris*) to (*Rome*)?"

"How many (*metres*) are there in a (*kilometre*)?"

"Where does (*sushi*) come from?"

"Who invented (*the telephone*)?"

"Who won (*the World Cup in 1998*)?"

"What's the biggest (*diamond*) in the world?"

b Answering questions

"I think ..."

"I'm not sure, but I think ..."

"I've no idea!"

Task

1 Work in teams of four or five. You are going to make up your own general knowledge quiz, using these categories:

- History   • Geography   • Science and Technology
- famous people   • sport   • food and drink   • other

▶ *Useful language a)*

2 In your teams, write at least **six** questions. Ask your teacher for any words or phrases you need.

3 Play your quiz game in teams. Each team gets two points for every question it answers correctly.

▶ *Useful language b)*

Optional writing

For homework, write some more questions to test **your teacher's** general knowledge. How many can he or she answer correctly?

Real life

Different ways of saying numbers

1 Match the numbers a–j with how you say them 1–10.

a 50 km/h   1 five thousand

b 500   2 five billion

c 505   3 five million

d 5,000   4 fifteen fifty-five

e 5.5   5 fifty kilometres per hour

f 50,000   6 five point five

g 500,000   7 five hundred thousand

h 5,000,000   8 fifty thousand

i 5,000,000,000   9 five hundred and five

j 1555 (year)   10 five hundred

2 📼 [11.5] Practise saying the numbers in the box. Then listen and check.

70	400	820	9,000	4.8	20,000
300,000		12,000,000	6,000,000,000		1,988

3 Write down:

a the approximate population of your town/city.

b the approximate price of a new car in your country.

c the approximate population of your country.

d the maximum prize in the national lottery.

e the year you were born.

f the approximate number of words on this page.

g the maximum speed limit in your country.

h how old your town/city is.

i the number of people in your school.

j the distance from your town/city to the coast.

(Don't worry if your numbers aren't exact.)

4 Compare your numbers in groups. Practise saying the different numbers.

Do you remember?

1 a) Write down three things you **can** do. (two true and one false). Write down three things you **can't** do. (two true and one false)

b) Read them to your partner. Can you guess the false ones?

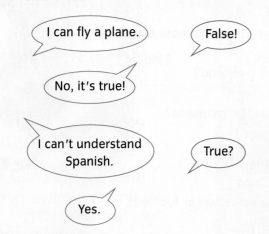

I can fly a plane.

False!

No, it's true!

I can't understand Spanish.

True?

Yes.

2 a) Complete the questions with a question word or phrase.

1 <u>How often</u> do you watch television?

2 .... of television programme do you like most?

3 .... is your favourite television actor or actress?

4 .... station (CNN, BBC World, MTV, etc.) do you like best?

5 .... films have you got on video?

b) Now ask your partner questions 1–5.

3 Put these questions in the correct order.

a) fast/type/you/How/can?
   How fast can you type?

b) Tokyo/long/Paul/How/did/in/live?

c) team/football/you/support/Which/do?

d) this/How/cost/much/does/book?

e) shops/the/far/are/How?

f) the/fast/to/How/you/can/get/airport?

g) dessert/would/What/you/like/for?

4 Write the answers in words, not numbers!

+ = plus   **−** = minus
✕ = multiplied by   **÷** = divided by

a) What is thirty thousand minus two thousand and seventy-two?
   Twenty-seven thousand, nine hundred and twenty-eight

b) What is one thousand, two hundred and eighty-four divided by twelve?

c) What is the year after the year two thousand?

d) What's six hundred and twenty-two thousand, three hundred and twenty-five plus fifty-nine thousand, two hundred and seventy-nine?

e) What's the speed limit on *city* roads in your country, or the country where you are studying?

f) What is sixty-six point six percent of a hundred and twenty?

5 How do you pronounce these international words in English? Mark the stress.

kilometre	metre	a billion	football
restaurant	television		

Practice

1 Write **six** sentences about the people in Language focus 1, Exercise 1 using *going to*.

On Saturday Val's going to pack for her holidays.

2 Look at pictures a–f carefully to see what the people are going to do.

- go swimming   e
- catch a plane   ☐
- meet his girlfriend ☐

- have a cigarette outside ☐
- take the dog for a walk   ☐
- go shopping   ☐

3 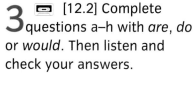 [12.2] Complete questions a–h with *are*, *do* or *would*. Then listen and check your answers.

a Are you going straight home after this lesson? If not, where ....are.... you going?

b .... you going to do any homework tonight? What .... you going to do?

c .... you want to watch TV this evening? .... you want to watch anything special?

d .... you going to have a busy weekend? What .... you like to do?

e .... you going out anywhere this week? If so, where .... you going?

f Are there any films that you .... like to see? Which ones?

g .... you want to buy anything special in the next few weeks? What?

h .... you want to go on holiday this year? Where .... you like to go?

Pronunciation

1 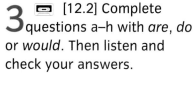 [12.3] Notice that *to* has a weak pronunciation in the middle of a sentence:

/tə/

Are you going to have a busy weekend?

/tə/

What do you want to do?

2 Listen again and practise the questions.

4 Work in pairs. Ask and answer questions a–h in Exercise 3.

Language focus 2

Suggestions and offers

 [12.4] What is the situation in the pictures? Put the two conversations in the correct order. Then listen and check. Practise with a partner.

- ☐ It's OK, I'll make it.
- ☐ No, I'll make it – you sit down.
- ☐ Good idea – shall I make some coffee?
- ☐ OK then – thanks.
- ☒ Let's stop for a break – this is really tiring!

(A)

- ☐ Shall I find out when it's on and what time it starts?
- ☐ How about that new one with Julia Roberts? I can't remember the name of it.
- ☐ Yes fine, what do you want to do?
- ☐ OK then – but which film?
- ☒ I'm really bored, shall we go out somewhere tonight?
- ☐ Yes, good idea.
- ☐ We could go and see a film.
- ☐ OK, if you like.

(B)

Grammar

1 a We make **suggestions** like this:
  Let's have a break.
  Shall we go out tonight?
  We could go to the cinema.
b How can the other person answer?

2 a We make offers like this:
  Shall I make some coffee?
  I'll make it
b How can the other person answer?

► *Language summary C/D page 148.*

Practice

 Work with a partner. Make as many conversations as you can, using sentences from A, B and C.

> **A**
> I'm really hungry/thirsty/tired/bored.
> It's really hot/cold/dark in here, isn't it?
> It's nearly midnight – I must go home!

> **B**
> Shall I make you a sandwich?
> Shall I take you home?
> Let's have a break.
> I'll turn on the heating/the light.
> Let's go and have lunch/a drink.
> We could go for a walk.
> Shall we call a taxi?
> I'll open/close the window.
> Shall I make some coffee?

> **C**
> Good idea!
> OK then.
> Yes, please, if that's OK.
> It's OK, I'll do it.

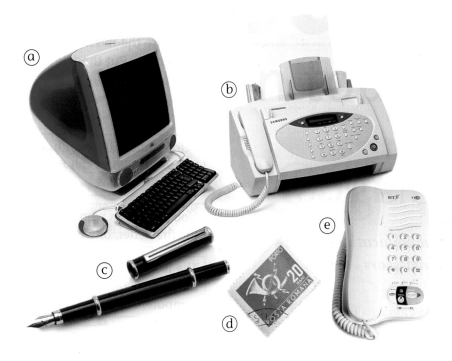

Vocabulary

Ways of communicating

1 MD Look at the objects in the pictures. Match the activities in the box with the objects.

> receive or send e-mails   leave a message   write a letter
> send a fax   surf the Internet   send cards   write a note
> buy (something) online   make calls

2 Use a phrase from the box to complete sentences a–i.

a   In many countries, it's normal to .... at New Year, or on birthdays.

b   If the person you want to speak to isn't at home when you phone, you can .... on the answering machine.

c   In the UK books and CDs are quite expensive; many people use computers and .... them ....

d   You can still find public telephones but many people nowadays prefer to use a mobile phone to ....

e   If you want to send a document quickly, and haven't got a computer, the best way is to ....

f   If you have a computer with a telephone connection, you can .... to keep in touch without paying a lot of money.

g   Brigitte wasn't there when I went to see her, so I decided to .... and leave it on her door.

h   Every night I like to .... for about an hour – you never know what interesting information you'll find on the web!

i   If you don't have a computer, you can always .... : it takes more time, but it's more personal.

Language focus 1

Present Perfect

MD Read about Caitlin Lewis. What's her job? What is surprising about her?

Caitlin Lewis, author of best–selling detective novels such as *Black Night* and *Death of a Stranger*, lives alone on the island of Tresco off the south coast of England. She's written sixteen novels and she's writing her seventeenth at the moment, but she doesn't have a computer and she's never sent a fax or an e-mail in her life!

'I've always used the same old typewriter which belonged to my mother. I think all this new technology is unnecessary. It's the ideas that are important.'

Grammar

1 Look at these sentences in the Present Perfect.
a *She's **written** sixteen novels.*
b *She's never **sent** an e-mail.*

We use the Present Perfect for actions in the past which are still true (or important) in the present. We don't say **when** the actions happened.

2 We form the Present Perfect with: **have** or **has** + past participle.

Notice how we form past participles:

Regular (= **verb** + **-ed**)
used

Irregular
written, sent

3 Complete the gaps with a sentence in the *I* form.
➕ *She's sent an e-mail.* I've sent an e-mail.
➖ *She hasn't sent an e-mail.* I..........................
❓ *Has she sent an e-mail?* ....

▶ **Language summary A page 148.**

Practice

1 [MD] Use your mini-dictionary to find the past participles of these irregular verbs:

be .... have ....
buy .... lose ....
see .... meet ....
make .... break ....

2 a) Write sentences about yourself. Use the list of verbs on page 150 to check irregular past participles.

a Write a letter in English
   I've never written a letter in English.
   I've written a few letters in English.
b Send an e-mail abroad
c Receive a fax
d Write a story
e Send a card at New Year
f Make an emergency call
g Lose an important letter
h Buy a book online
i Visit a cybercafé

b) Speak to your partner. Are your answers the same or different?

3 [MD] **a)** Use the words to write at least six questions.

go to	the USA/Paris/a rock concert
	Have you ever been to Paris?
see	a real tiger/an opera/ the film *'Casablanca'*
write	a poem/a love letter/a very angry letter
lose	a lot of money/your identity card/ your English homework
meet	a person from Britain/a famous person/your teachers husband or wife
break	your arm/your leg/a promise

b) Work in groups of three. Use your questions to find **two** things that you have done that your partners have not.

Have you ever seen a tiger?

No, I haven't.

Me neither.

Advertise a local tourist attraction

Preparation for task

1 Read the advertisement about Adam Square from the local tourist office. Put the questions in the correct space.

a How do you get there?
b What can you do there?
c Where is it?
d Are there any other attractions nearby?

2 Say four things that visitors can do in Adam Square.

> They can walk around the shops.

Welcome to the town's greatest attraction!

Adam Square!

(1) .... ?

Adam Square is right in the centre of the town.

(2) .... ?

You can walk around the shops or you can have a cup of coffee. Try one of the fashionable cafés such as 'Domino'. For a good meal, go to Pete's Pizzeria: we recommend Pete's Special Pizza ... it's really good and not too expensive!

(3) .... ?

Walk along Rose Way and visit Prince's Park – it's perfect for children.

Take a number 32 bus to the Market Square: you can buy fruit and vegetables, or souvenirs. The market is open every day except Sunday.

If you like historic buildings, visit the Church of St. Nicholas. It's nearly 500 years old.

(4) .... ?

Come to the Square on foot or by bicycle – you can't drive in Adam Square.

To get to Adam Square from the city bus station:
Come out of the station, and turn left. Walk along Via Pazzini. Go past the Tourist Information Office and you're at Adam Square.
Or if you're rich, take a taxi!

Task

1 Work in a group. Think of a place in your town or a nearby town which is interesting for tourists. Make notes about:

- where it is.
- what you can do there.
- other interesting places to go which are nearby.
- where to have a walk.
- old buildings/monuments.
- how to get there from the bus/railway station.

2 Make up a poster like the one on page 120 OR record your description onto cassette. You can use the same questions as the ones in the advertisement.

Do you remember?

1 Complete the words.

a)	It goes up!	h i l l
b)	It's near the sea.	b _ _ _ _
c)	You can look at pictures here.	a _ _ g _ _ _ _ _ _
d)	Kings and queens lived here.	c _ _ _ _ _
e)	There are a lot of shops together here.	s _ _ _ _ _ _ _ c _ _ _ _ _
f)	You can watch football here.	s _ _ _ _ _ _
g)	You can play football here!	p _ _ _

2 Look at the sentences below. Tick them (✓) if they are true about your city or town and change them if they are not true.

a) In parks you can walk on the grass.

   No, in public parks you can't walk on the grass.

b) You can't eat or drink on trains.

c) You have to stop your car when people walk across the street.

d) You can smoke in restaurants.

e) You can't park your car in the town centre.

f) You have to ride your bicycle on the pavement.

g) You can't take a dog into a shop.

h) You don't have to pay to go into a museum or an art gallery.

3 Write two prepositions of movement for each noun.

a) drive ..along../ .... a river   e) walk ..../ .... the stairs

b) walk ..../ .... a building   f) get ..../ .... a car

c) drive ..../ .... an airport g) run ..../ .... a park

d) go ..../ .... a road

4 Is the pronunciation of the bold letters the same (S) or different (D)?

a	hi**ll**	li**br**ary	D
b	mu**s**eum	**s**treet	
c	**ai**rport	sq**ua**re	
d	s**t**atue	s**t**eps	
e	buildin**g**	brid**g**e	
f	s**t**adium	**p**ark	

Practice

1 MD **a)** Match the verbs in the box with the pictures.

b) Make sentences using the ideas in the pictures and the phrases in the box.

> borrow   go sightseeing
> look for   improve
> pass her exams   study
> find a better job   use
> go to a good university

a Jo went to the library …
   to study for her
   exams.
   ....
   ....

b Paolo came to London …
   ....
   ....

c Selina needs to work hard …
   ....
   ....

2 Why do people do these things? Tell a partner.

a go to the mountains
b use a dictionary
c use a credit card
d catch a bus
e go to the supermarket
f go abroad
g use a computer

> Why do people go to the mountains?

> to go skiing

> to go walking

①

Jo

②

Paolo

③

Selina

Listening

An expert talks about the English language

John Summers

1 Look at the four statements. Which ideas do you think are true?

a English is an easy language to learn.
true/false/not sure

b The pronunciation and spelling of English are quite easy.
true/false/not sure

c More people study English than any other language around the world.
true/false/not sure

d Half the people in the world speak English now.
true/false/not sure

2 🔲 [15.3] Listen to John Summers. Are your ideas the same?

3 Listen again and answer questions a–g.

PART A

a How many forms of the verb are there in Latin?

b How many forms of the verb are there in English?

c What forms of the verb *go* does he give?

d What is more difficult in English than in some other languages?

PART B

e There are more people learning English in China than ....

f About how many people are learning English all over the world now?

g When will 50% of the world's population speak English, according to some experts?

Reading

1 In what ways is your language easier or more difficult than English? Why?
Think about these areas:

- vocabulary.
- spelling.
- pronunciation.
- grammar.

2 Read the text 'Easy English?' Which paragraph:

a is about a man who invented a new English with a smaller vocabulary? ☐

b is about a man who tried to change the spelling of English? ☐

c introduces the topic? ☐

d is about how e-mail is changing English? ☐

e is about a form of English which people use at sea? ☐

Easy English?

"I'D LIKE A LARGE GREEN FRUIT WITH THE FORM OF AN EGG WHICH HAS A SWEET RED INSIDE AND GOOD TASTE"

1 English is an important global language – but that doesn't mean it's easy to learn. Many experts have tried to make English easier for students to learn ... but they weren't always successful.

2 In 1930, Professor C.K. Ogden of Cambridge University invented Basic English ... it had only 850 words (and just eighteen verbs!), and Ogden said most people could learn it in just thirty hours ... The problem was that those people who learned Basic English could write and say simple messages ... but they couldn't understand the answers in 'real' English! It was also impossible to explain a word which wasn't in the Basic English word list; so if you wanted a water melon, you asked for 'a large green fruit with the form of an egg, which has a sweet red inside and a good taste.'

3 R.E. Zachrisson, a university professor in Sweden, decided that the biggest problem for learners of English was spelling ... so he invented a language called Anglic. Anglic was similar to English but with much simpler spelling. 'Father' became 'faadher', 'new' became 'nue' ... and 'years' became 'yeerz'. Sadly, Anglic never became popular.

4 Even easier is the language which ships' captains use: it's called 'Seaspeak'. Seaspeak uses a few simple phrases for every possible situation. In 'Seaspeak', for example, you don't say 'I'm sorry, what did you say?' or 'I didn't understand, can you repeat that?' ... it's just 'Say again.' No more grammar!

5 In the age of computers and international communication through the Internet, who knows? ... a new form of English might appear. A large number of the world's e-mail messages are in English and include examples of NetLingo like O.I.C. (Oh, I see!) and T.T.Y.L. (Talk to you later). In another fifty years English as we know it might not exist ... we will probably all speak fluent Internetish!!

3 Ask and answer these questions with a partner.

a When did Professor Ogden invent Basic English? How many words did it have?

b Why did Professor Zachrisson invent Anglic? What happened to it?

c Why is Seaspeak easier than ordinary English?

d What is 'Internetish', do you think?

e Is it a good idea to learn Anglic or Seaspeak instead of English?

f How would you like to change English to make it easier?

Language focus 2

Modal verbs for possibility: *might* and *will*

a) Tick (✓) the statements if you agree and write a cross (✗) if you don't agree.

a Soon, nearly everyone will speak English.

b People won't learn Latin any more.

c English might not be the global language in a hundred years – it might be Chinese or Japanese instead.

d Some 'smaller' languages will disappear.

b) Compare your answers with the class.

Grammar

might and will
a Number the sentences 1–4 .
(1 = most possible)
□ *English <u>might not</u> be the global language.*
□ *English won't be the global language.*
□ *English will be the global language.*
□ *English might be the global language.*

b <u>Underline</u> the verbs of possibility.

c Notice these short forms:
They 'll (= will) disappear.
They won't (= will not) disappear.
▶ *Language summary B page 149.*

Practice

1 Complete each sentence. Use *might, might not* and *'ll (will)*.

a If you work hard, you .... *(pass your exams)*.

b In the future, people .... *(go to university)*: they .... *(study at home)* using their computer.

c Tom isn't sure what he wants to do when he leaves secondary school: he .... *(go to university)* or he .... *(go abroad)* for a year.

d Why not do a course in Japanese? You never know – you .... *(need)* to speak it one day!

e Deniz doesn't like her teacher: she thinks she .... *(change)* her class soon.

f Some teachers are worried that one day computers .... *(take)* their jobs.

2 Complete these sentences so that they are true for you. You can write about:

• where you live.

• getting married or not.

• being rich.

• speaking English.

• other ideas.

a Next winter I might go..to..Austria..

b Next summer I might ....

c Next year I'll ....

d In ten years' time I might ....

e I might not ever ....

f I won't ever ....

3 Work with a partner. Talk about your answers.

Next winter I might go to Austria.

Oh, why?

Because I'd like to go skiing.

Find the right course

Preparation for task

1 These three students are choosing a course at The West Midlands College of Technology (W.E.M.C.O.T.). Read the notes about each student.

Clara

19 years old.

Left school last year.

Not sure what job she'd like to do – but she doesn't want to work in an office.

Hobbies: playing football, swimming, travelling and meeting people.

Taka

From Japan. 27 years old.

Works as a fashion designer.

Going to stay in England for one year.

Enjoys art and photography.

Wants to learn more about computers.

Ben

18 years old

Plays in a rock band with his friends.

Enjoys drama.

Likes computers.

Wants to be rich and famous one day!

2 **[MD]** Read about the different courses and answer questions a–c.

a Which course is for people who want to work in sports centres?

b Which course teaches photography?

c Which courses are one-year courses?

Leisure and Tourism

For people interested in a career in tourism.

• Marketing and promotion
• Customer service
• Information technology

The course is one year, full-time. You must be at least 16 years old, with …

Sports Studies

For people who would like to work in sports/leisure centres, swimming pools, etc.

• Health and safety
• Sport coaching
• Fitness and diet

This is a two year, full-time course open to people over 16 years of age …

choose your
course

Basic Information Technology

For people who would like to work in business or industry.

• Computing for business and industry
• Using information technology
• Programming and software

This course is one-year full-time. You must be at least 16, with an interest in computers …

Art and Design

A course to help you find work in the fashion and media industries. Subjects include:

• Clothes design
• Using computer software
• Photography

Two years, full-time.
Students must be at least 16 …

Performing Arts

Includes music, dance, drama in the first year. In the second year, students can choose special subjects such as:

• Singing
• Directing
• Marketing

Students must be at least 16 at the time of entry. The course is two years, full time.

Task

1 **a)** Which course do you think each of the students will choose?

Clara

Course: ....

Why? ....

Taka

Course: ....

Why? ....

Ben

Course: ....

Why? ....

b) Compare your answers in pairs.

2 [15.4] Listen to the three students talking about which courses they chose. Did they choose the same courses as you?

Communication activities ....

Module 7: Real life, Exercise 4, page 63

Student A

1   Read the sentences 1–5 to Student B. Student B gives you the dates or times to complete the sentences.

George Washington

1   George Washington was President of the USA ....

2   There is a U.S. national holiday on his birthday, ...

3   He was born ....

4   He signed the Declaration of Independence ....

5   He died ....

2   Listen to Student B's sentences. Tell Student B the dates or years to complete the sentences.

Christopher Columbus

1   .... fifteenth century.

2   .... on October 11th.

3   .... in 1451.

4   .... on August 3rd, 1492.

5   .... on May 20th, 1506.

Module 9: Real life, Exercise 4, page 80

Student A

1   Go to the general store and try to buy these things.

> shampoo
> a cake
> film for camera
> baseball cap
> postcards

2   You are the shop assistant. Look at the information and serve the customer.

Prices
bananas £1.50 a kilo
stamps Europe 30 pence   Other 55 pence
tee-shirts small £9.99 medium £10.99 large £11.99
toothpaste
You don't sell batteries.

Module 1: Practice, Exercise 1, page 12

Celine Dion – singer – Canada – married – born 1968

Module 11: Reading, Exercise 2, page 91

Wolves attack and kill more than twenty people every year.

This sentence is false.

Module 10: Task, Exercise 1, page 87

1 Add **ten** of the things in the box to Picture B below. Do not show your picture to your partner!

> the sun rain clouds headphones
> glasses sunglasses a baseball cap
> a pony tail a mobile phone trainers
> long hair short hair a large ice cream
> a piece of cake a cup of coffee a cigarette
> some happy faces some unhappy faces

2 When you finish your picture, turn back to page 87.

Module 9, Real life, Exercise 4, page 80

Student B

1 You are the shop assistant in a general store. Look at the information and serve the customer.

Prices
film *24 £4.50 36 £5.00*
postcards *25 pence each*
cakes *60 pence or £5.00*
baseball caps *small £3.00 medium £3.50 large £4.50*
You don't sell shampoo.

2 Go to a general store and try to buy these things.

stamps
bananas
batteries for camera
toothpaste
a tee shirt

Communication activities

Consolidation 6–10: Listening; song, Exercise E, page 89

Return to Sender

1   Listen to the song and complete the gaps.

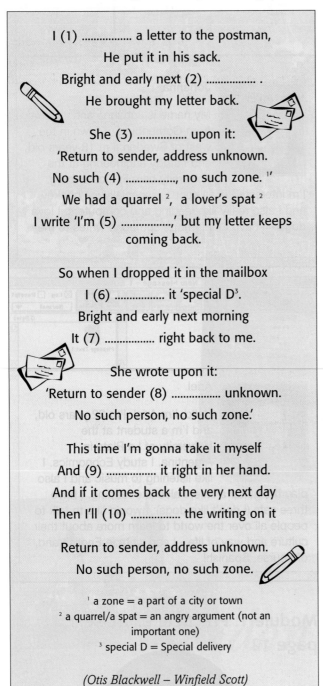

I (1) .... a letter to the postman,
He put it in his sack.
Bright and early next (2) ....
He brought my letter back.

She (3) .... upon it:
'Return to sender, address unknown.
No such (4) ...., no such zone. [1]'
We had a quarrel [2], a lover's spat [2]
I write 'I'm (5) ....,' but my letter keeps
coming back.

So when I dropped it in the mailbox
I (6) .... it 'special D[3].
Bright and early next morning
It (7) .... right back to me.

She wrote upon it:
'Return to sender (8) .... unknown.
No such person, no such zone.'

This time I'm gonna take it myself
And (9) .... it right in her hand.
And if it comes back the very next day
Then I'll (10) .... the writing on it

Return to sender, address unknown.
No such person, no such zone.

[1] a zone = a part of a city or town
[2] a quarrel/a spat = an angry argument (not an
important one)
[3] special D = Special delivery

(Otis Blackwell – Winfield Scott)

2   Now check your answers with Student B.

Module 1: Practice, Exercise 1, page 12

*Michael Schumacher – sportsman –
Germany – married – born 1969*

Module 4: Task, Exercise 1, page 36

Student A

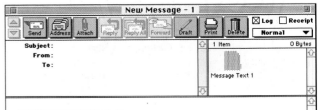

Peter

My name's Peter and I am 23 years old. I come from Singapore, and I speak two languages: English and Mandarin Chinese. I have many hobbies: my interests are writing and listening to music; playing softball; going to the movies; and having fun with my friends. I also like cooking. I want to make friends all over the world.

Rachel

Hi! It's good to meet you! I'm Rachel, and I come from Texas, in the United States of America. I'm 16 years old. I love to play tennis and basketball, and I also like to read: and I really, really, really love music – I play the drums in my school band, and I also sing! My favourite singer of all time is Mariah Carey. Do you like her? Please write to me!

Language summary

Module 1

A The verb be

1 Positive, negative and question forms

Positive form	I'm (= am) he/she/it's (= is) you/we/ they're (= are)	from England. twenty years old. Spanish.
Negative form	I'm not (= am not) he/she/it isn't (= is not) you/we/they aren't (= are not)	American. from Poland. Italian.
Question form	Am I Is he/she/it Are you/we/they	from the USA? British? from Japan?
Short answers	Yes, I am Yes, he/she/it is Yes, you/we/ they are	No, I'm not No, he/she/it isn't No, you/we/ they aren't

> **REMEMBER!**
> We do not use the short form of the verb in short answers.
>
> Yes, I **am**.   ~~Yes, I'm.~~
>
> Yes, she **is**.   ~~Yes, she's.~~
>
> Yes, they **are**.   ~~Yes, they're.~~

2 Questions with question words

What	's are	your job? your names?
Where	's are	Alain from? your friends?
How old	's are	Richard? you?
Who	's are	your teacher? they?

B Personal pronouns and possessive adjectives

Personal pronoun	Possessive adjective	
I	my	*My* name's James Taylor.
you	your	*How old is **your** car?*
he	his	***His** address is 6 Leyton Avenue.*
she	her	*What's **her** telephone number?*
it	its	***Its** full name is the British Broadcasting Corporation (BBC).*
we	our	***Our** children are six and eight years old.*
they	their	*What's **their** e-mail address?*

> **REMEMBER!**
>
> 1   **His** *is for a man.*   **His** *name's* **Paul**.
>   **Her** *is for a woman.*   **Her** *name's* **Anna**.
>
> 2   **Your** *is for singular*   *What's **your** name?*   **Aldona**.
>   *and plural.*   *What are **your** names?*   **Julio** *and* **Maria**.

C a and an: indefinite articles with jobs

We use *a/an* for jobs.
Use **an** before vowels (a,e,i,o,u)   **an** *actor,* **an** *architect,* **an** *engineer*

Use **a** before consonants (b,c,d,f,g,h, …)   **a** *politician,* **a** *doctor,* **a** *manager*

D Capital letters

We use capital letters for:
– names: *Lara Croft, Queen Elizabeth*
– countries: *China, the United States*
– nationalities: *Brazilian, Greek*
– roads: *23 Stamford Road, Fifth Avenue*
– towns/cities: *New York, Istanbul*

Module 2

A this, that, these and those

	Here		There	
singular	this	(book)	that	(book)
plural	these	(books)	those	(books)

Other examples:
*Mr Thomson, **this is** Jane Dunn.*   ***These** apples **are** good.*
***Are these** your keys?*   *Yes, they are. Thanks.*
*Who **are those** people?*

> **REMEMBER!**
> *In the answer we usually use* **it's** *or* **they're**.
>
> What's this/that?   **It's** a credit card.
>
> What are these/those?   **They're** videos.

B Nouns: singular and plural

Singular	Plural	Spelling
a credit card	*credit cards*	+ *s*
a watch	*watches*	+ *es* (after *ch,sh,s,x,z*)
a family	*families*	+ *ies* (consonant + *y* → *ies*)

C Adjectives

Adjectives:
– go **before** nouns.   *a comfortable car*   ~~a car comfortable~~
– do **not** change.   *blue eyes*   ~~eyes blue~~
– do **not** use *and*.   *a fantastic new motorbike*   *a fantastic ~~and~~ new motorbike*

D *a* and *an* with singular nouns and adjectives

1   We use *a / an* + singular nouns.
a *diary,* **a** *job,* **a** *tourist,* **a** *photo,* **an** *apple,* **an** *address,* **an** *e-mail*
(but **a** *university*)

2   We use *a / an* + adjectives and singular nouns.
a *new car,* **a** *white cat,* **a** *French cigarette,* **an** *English teacher,*
an *African country*

E *have got*

1 Positive, negative and question forms

Positive form	I/you/we/they **'ve got** (= have got) he/she/it**'s got** (= has got)	a new telephone number.
		a television.
Negative form	I/you/we/they **haven't got** (= have not got) he/she/it **hasn't got** (= has not got)	a cassette player.
		a mobile phone.
Question form	**Have** I/you/ we/they **got**	an English– Portuguese dictionary?
	Has he/she/it **got**	a CD player?
Short answers	Yes, I/you/ we/they **have.** Yes, he/she/it **has.**	No, I/you/we/ they **haven't** No, he/she/it **hasn't.**

We use *have got* for:
a   possession
I've got *a new credit card.*   *My school***'s got** *twenty five computers.*
b   relationships
*José***'s got** *a new girlfriend.*   *Barbara and Nicholas* **have got** *three children.*

> **REMEMBER!**
> 1   **He's** American. *(he's = he* **is***)*   **He's** got an American car.
> *(he's = he* **has***)*
>
> 2   *We do not use the short form of the verb in short answers.*
>
> Yes, I **have.**   ~~Yes, I've.~~
>
> Yes, he **has.**   ~~Yes, he's.~~

2 Question forms with question word(s)

| **How many** | *brothers* | has Elena got? |
| **What** | *answer* | have you got for question 2? |

F Possessive *'s* and *of*

1   We use a person + *'s* for possession.
Jane's brother   ~~the brother of Jane~~
Patrick's computer
His friend's car
My father's name

2   We usually use *of* before things or places.
– *a picture* **of** *a car*   ~~a car's picture~~
– *the Queen* **of** *England*   ~~England's Queen~~
– *the Tower* **of** *London*   ~~London's Tower~~

Module 3

A Present Simple *I, you, we* and *they* forms

Positive form	I/you/we/they	**live** in a big city. **drink** coffee.
Negative form	I/you/we/they	**don't like** coffee. **don't live** in a flat.
Question form	Do I/you/we/they	**speak** French? **study** at university?
Short answers	Yes, I/we/you/they No, I/we/you/they	**do.** **don't.**

We use the Present Simple for:
a   things which are generally / always true.
Judy and I **live** *with our parents.*   *Mel and Jo* **don't speak** *Russian.*
b   habits and routines.
We **go** *shopping on Saturday.*   *I* **study** *English in the evening.*

> **REMEMBER!**
> *We do not use the full verb in the short answer.*
>
> Do you like pop music?   Yes, I **do.**   ~~Yes, I like.~~
>
> No, I **don't.**   ~~No, I don't like.~~

Module 4

A Present simple *he, she* and *it*

Positive form	he/she/it	**likes** dogs. **loves** chocolate.
Negative form	he/she/it	**doesn't like** (= does not like) my brother. **doesn't eat** (= does not eat) fish.
Question form	**Does** he/she/ **Does** it	**live** with you? **rain** a lot in Brazil?
Short answers	Yes, he/she/it No, he/she/it	**does.** **doesn't.**

> **REMEMBER!**
>
> 1 For negative and question forms:
>
>   Patrick do**es**n't likes meat.
>   Do**es** Vanessa likes cooking?
>
> 2 We do not use the full verb in the answer.
>
>   Yes, she **does**.   ~~Yes, she likes.~~
>   No, she **doesn't**.   ~~No, she doesn't like.~~

Ⓑ *like, love* and *hate* + *...ing*

After *like / love / hate*, we use a plural noun or verb + *...ing.*
– I hate spider**s**.
– She doesn't like crowd**s**.
– Do you like dog**s**?

– Joe likes play**ing** golf.
– We don't like fly**ing**.
– Do they like play**ing** computer games?

Ⓒ Present Simple: spelling

The spelling rules for *he*, *she* and *it*:

Verb Most verbs	Rule add **s**	Beth come**s** from the USA. Paul want**s** a new car.
Ends in a consonant + *y*	change **y** to **ies**	This airline fl**ies** to Slovenia.
Ends in: *ch , sh , s, x, z*	add **es**	Andrew watch**es** a lot of videos. Fran finish**es** work at six.
do and *go*	add **es**	My manager go**es** home at eleven! Pat do**es** all the housework.
have	**has**	He **has** breakfast at seven.

Ⓓ Present Simple questions: *he, she* and *it*

What	does	he/she/it	think of Japan? like eating?
Where	does	Juan	come from? live? work?
What time	does	the class Anna	start? go to work?

Ⓔ Adverbs of frequency

We use frequency adverbs and the Present Simple to say *how often* we do something.

```
never   not often            often      always
0%          sometimes      usually   100%
```

a We usually put the adverb *before* the verb.
  My children **sometimes** watch a video on Sunday evening.
  Nicolas **never** goes to school on Saturday.
  I **don't often** visit my brother's family.
  I **don't usually** like pasta.

b We put the adverb *after* the verb *be*.
  English people are **usually** very friendly.
  The winters are **sometimes** very cold.
  The weather isn't **always** good.
  I'm **not often** home in the evening.

Module 5

Ⓐ *most, a lot of, some, not many*

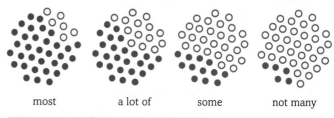

most   a lot of   some   not many

Most A lot of Some Not many	people	drive to work.

Ⓑ Definite, indefinite and zero articles

1 Indefinite article

We use *a* or *an*:
a with jobs.
  I'm **an** artist
b with a singular noun to mean 'one'.
  We have **a** real problem.
c with these phrases
  a lot of/**a** long time

2 Definite article

We use *the*:
a with times of day.
  in **the** morning/afternoon
  (BUT **at** night)
b with these phrases
  in **the** city centre
  on **the** right/left

3 Zero article

We do **not** use *a, an* or *the*:

a with towns and cities.	I'm from Boston.
b with most countries.	Lyon is in France. (BUT **the** United States, **the** United Kingdom, **the** Czech Republic)
c with '*by*' + a means of transport.	by bus/car/train
d with times + days.	at one o'clock on Monday
e with these phrases.	go to work/at home most people

C can and can't

Positive form	I/you/he/she/it/we/they	can go by train. can take a long time.
Negative form	I/you/he/she/it/ we/they	can't (= cannot) go by bus
Question form	Can	I/you/he/she/ it/we/they	travel by bus?

1 We use *can* to say that it is possible to do something.
   *You **can** take a train from Paddington Station to Heathrow.*

2 We use *can't* to say it is impossible to do something.
   *We **can't** take a taxi because we've only got £20.*

> **REMEMBER!**
> a We always use the base form of the verb after can.
>
>   *You **can eats** Chinese food in the city centre.*
>
> b We don't use do or does to make the question form.
>
>   ***Can you find** taxis in the street?*   ~~Do you can find taxis in the street?~~

Module 6

A Countable and uncountable nouns

Countable noun	Uncountable noun
egg apple book CD	milk butter money music

1 We can use countable nouns in the singular or plural.
   *Have you got **a** cat? Do you like cats?*

2 Uncountable nouns do **not** have a plural.
   Do you like classical music~~s~~?
Note: A dictionary says if a noun is countable or uncountable.

> **REMEMBER!**
> a Bread, toast, cake, milk, fruit juice, water, coffee, tea ...
>   are all uncountable, but we can talk about:
>   **a piece of** bread/toast/cake
>   **a glass of** milk/fruit juice/water
>   **a cup of** coffee/tea
>
> b We can also talk about **a** coffee, (= a cup of coffee)
>   and **two** teas ....

B there is and there are

	singular	plural
Positive form	There's a cup.	There are six plates.
Negative form	There isn't a bottle of milk.	There aren't two cups.
Question form	Is there a glass of orange juice?	Are there six glasses?
Short answers	Yes, there is. No, there isn't.	Yes, there are. No, there aren't.

C some and any

	singular countable noun	plural countable noun	uncountable noun
+	There's **an** apple.	There are **some** grapes.	There's **some** soup.
−	There isn't **a** bowl.	There aren't **any** glasses. There are **no** glasses.	There isn't **any** water. There's **no** water.
?	Is there **a** cinema?	Are there **any** shops?	Is there **any** money?

1 a We use *some* in the positive when we don't say exactly how many or how much.
      *Have **some** grapes!*
      *There's **some** soup and bread for lunch.*
      *I'd like **some** carrots please.*

   b *Some* = a small number/a small amount
      some onions   a lot of onions
      some money   a lot of money

2 We usually use *any* or *no* in negatives with plural and uncountable nouns.

I have**n't** got **any** money.	= I've got **no** money.
There are**n't any** e-mails.	= There are **no** e-mails.
There is**n't any** time.	= There's **no** time.

3 We usually use *any* in questions with plurals and uncountables.
   *Have you got **any** brothers or sisters?*
   *Are there **any** buses at night?*
   *Is there **any** meat in this soup?*

> **REMEMBER!**
>
> With plural and uncountable nouns:
>
> a We can also use some in these questions:
>
>   **Would you like some** cheese/coffee/grapes?
>   **Have you got some** grapes/mineral water?
>
> b We usually use some in this question:
>
>   **Can I have some** wine/cake/oranges?

D Questions with how much? and how many?

1 We use *how many* with countable plural nouns.
   ***How many** brothers/children/oranges have you got?*
   ***How many** cigarettes does Paul smoke every day?*

2 We use *how much* with uncountable nouns.
   ***How much** rice/milk/money have we got?*
   ***How much** coffee does Elena drink in a week?*

3 *How much/how many* and *there is/there are*:
   We use *there are* with countable plural nouns.
   We use *there is* with uncountable nouns.

How many teachers **are there** in your school?	**There are** about twenty, I think.
How much sugar **is there** in this cake?	It's okay. **There's** not much.

> **REMEMBER!**
> We use how much to ask about prices.
>
> **How much** is it/this/that?   How much are they/these/those?
> **How much** does it cost?   How much do they cost?
>
> It's £10.   They're £50.

Module 7

Ⓐ Past Simple: *was* and *were*

Positive form	I/he/she/it you/we/they	was at home. were at home.
Negative form	I/he/she/it **wasn't** (= **was not**) you/we they **weren't** (= **were not**)	at school. at school.
Question form	**Was** I/he /she/it **Were** you/we/they	friendly?
Short answers	Yes, I/he/she/it **was** Yes, you/we/they **were**.	No, he/she/it **wasn't**. No, you/we/ they **weren't**.

> **REMEMBER**
> I was born in 1985.   ~~I born in 1985.~~   ~~I was borned in 1985.~~

Ⓑ Past Simple: regular and irregular verbs

1 Regular verbs

Usually we add -ed to the verb.
I/you/he/she/it/we/they work**ed**, want**ed**, finish**ed**, listen**ed**, watch**ed**, play**ed**

Other spelling rules:

Verb	Rule	
Ends in **-e** (*live*)	+ **d**	She live**d** in France
Ends in a consonant + vowel + consonant (*stop*)	double the final consonant	He stop**ped** work at 5.30.
Ends in consonant + y (*study*)	Change **y** to **ied**	I stud**ied** economics.

2 Irregular verbs

Many common verbs have an irregular past form:
go – went, have – had, meet – met, know – knew.

▶ **Verb list on page 150.**

We use the Past Simple to talk about:
– a finished single action in the past.
My parents **met** *in 1960.*
The film **started** *at 7.30.*
– a finished state in the past.
Kate **had** *a happy childhood.*
We **lived** *in a small city.*
– a repeated action in the past.
She always **telephoned** *me on Monday.*
They **went** *swimming every day.*

When we use the Past Simple, we often **say** the time of the action: *in 1960, at 7.30, on Monday.*

Ⓒ Past time phrases

1 *in*

in	+ year	in 1999
	+ decade	in the 1980s
	+ century	in the 20th century
	+ month	in July

2 *ago*

ago = before now
The film began ten minutes **ago**.
She died fifteen years **ago**.

3 *from ... to...*

I worked for the company **from** *1994* **to** *2000.*
The lesson was **from** *half past six* **to** *eight.*

4 *on* + day

I played tennis with Luis **on Friday**.

> **REMEMBER**
> We do not use a preposition (in, on, from, ...) with:
>
> last   We watched television **last** night.
>
> yesterday   Manuel phoned me **yesterday**.

Ⓓ Ordinal numbers

1st	→	first	11th	→	eleventh
2nd	→	second	12th	→	twelfth
3rd	→	third	13th	→	thirteenth
4th	→	fourth	20th	→	twentieth
5th	→	fifth	21st	→	twenty-first
6th	→	sixth	22nd	→	twenty-second
7th	→	seventh	30th	→	thirtieth
8th	→	eighth	33rd	→	thirty-third
9th	→	ninth	40th	→	fortieth
10th	→	tenth	100th	→	hundredth

We use ordinal numbers:
– for dates: *December 25th:*
                         December the twenty-fifth.
– for floors in a building: *The classroom is on the third floor.*
– as an adjective: *She's Paolo's second wife.*
                         My first car was a Fiat Uno.

Module 8

Ⓐ Past Simple: negative

I/you/he/she/it/ we/they	didn't (= did not)	start come	at 10.00. to the park.

> **REMEMBER!**
> We use didn't + the base form of the verb. Regular and irregular verbs are the same.
>
> She **didn't go** shopping.   She didn't ~~went~~ shopping.

Ⓑ Past Simple questions

Question form		
Did **Did**	you/he/she	walk to work today? sleep well?

Short answers	
Yes, I/we/you/he	**did.**
No, I/we/you/he	**didn't**

2 *Want to* + verb; *would like to* + verb

1 *Want to* + verb
Positive form

I/you/we/they	want to	eat
he/she/it	wants to	eat

Question form

Do you	want to	eat?
Does he		

Yes, I **do**	Yes, he **does**
No, I **don't**	No, he **doesn't**

Negative form

I/you/we/they	**don't**	want to	eat.
he/she /it	**doesn't**		

2 *Would like to* + verb
Positive form

I/you/he/she/it/we/they	**'d like to**	eat.

Negative form

I/you/we/it/we/they	**wouldn't like to**	eat.

Question form

Would	I/you/he/she/it/we/they	**like to**	eat.

a   We use **want** and **would** like to talk about our wishes.
   Would like is usually more polite.
   *I **want to** see the manager!*   *I'**d like to** book a room, please.*

b   In the negative we don't often use *wouldn't like to*. We prefer
   don't want to.
   *I **don't want to** go out tonight.*   ~~I wouldn't like to go out tonight~~.

B Future time expressions

These are some common expressions we use when we are talking about future plans and intentions:

I'm going to see Patricia	*today, tonight* *this ... morning/afternoon/evening/* *weekend/month/year/summer* *tomorrow,* *tomorrow ... morning/afternoon/* *evening/night* *next ... week/month/year/summer*

C Suggestions with *let's, shall we, we could* + verb

Suggestion		Positive response	Negative response
Let's (= let us) **Shall we** **We could**	*watch a video?* *go dancing.*	*Good idea!* *Yes, fine.* *Yes, sure.* *Yes, okay.*	*Oh no!* (+ reason)

D Offers with *shall I?* and *I'll* + verb

Offer		Positive response	Negative response
Shall I	*order a pizza?*	*Good idea!*	*Oh no!* (+ reason)
I'll	*make some coffee.*	*Yes, please, if that's okay.* *Fine/okay/sure/ thanks.* *That's very kind of you.*	

Module 13

A Present Perfect

Positive form			
I/you/we/they	've (= *have*)		
he/she/it	's (= *has*)		met Anne before.

Negative form			
I/you/we/they	haven't		
he/she/it	hasn't		met Anne before.

Question form			
Have	I/you/we/they		
Has	he/she/it		met Anne before?

Short answers					
Yes,	I/you / we/they he/she/it	have has	No,	I/you / we/they he /she/it	haven't. hasn't.

1   We form the Present Perfect with *have/has* + the past participle of the verb.
   a   Regular past participles are the same as the past form and end in *-ed*: *used, finished, tried.*
   b   Many verbs have irregular past participles: *seen, been, had, done.*
   ▶ *Verb list page 150.*

2   We use the Present Perfect to talk about something that has (or hasn't) happened in the past. We don't say any specific time but we mean 'in my life up to now'.
   I've seen this film (before).
   She's had ten different jobs (in her life).
   They haven't been to the United States (before).
   He's never tried Thai food (before).

> **REMEMBER**
>
> Ever = *in your life up to now. We use ever to ask about something unusual.*
>
> ~~Have you ever watched TV?~~   *(Watching TV is common)*
>
> *Have you ever won a competition?*

B Definite, indefinite and zero articles

1 Zero article

We use zero article (Ø) with plural nouns or with uncountable nouns.

*Jane loves **children**.*
***Meat** is good for you.*

We use it to speak about things in general.

2 Indefinite article

We use *a / an* before a countable singular noun.

*I'm staying in **a** hotel in Bangkok.*

a / an = one, but we don't know which one,
or we use *a / an* when this is the first time we are speaking about something.

3 Definite article

We use *the* before nouns when it is clear that the speaker is talking about something specific or something which we know.

***The children** are in bed.*	= the children in my family / my children;
***The meat** is fantastic!*	= we know which meat, (the meat that I am eating now)
*I'm going back to **the hotel** soon.*	= we know which hotel because we spoke about it before

Module 14

A *have to* and *don't have to*

Positive form			
I/you/we/they he/she /it	have to has to		leave.
Negative form			
I/you/we/they he/she/it	don't doesn't	have to	leave.
Question form			
Do	I/you/we/they		have to go?
Does	he/she /it		
Short answers			
Yes,	I/you/ we/they	do.	Yes, he /she/it does.
No,		don't.	No, doesn't

1 We use *have to* when it is necessary or obligatory to do something.
*You **have to** drive on the left in Britain.*

2 We use *don't have to* when it is not necessary to do something, but you can if you want.
*You don't **have to** come to the party if you don't want to.*

> **REMEMBER**
> When it is **not** okay or it is prohibited to do something we use **can't**.
>
> *You can't smoke in the classroom* ~~You don't have to smoke in the classroom.~~

B *can* and *can't*

We use *can* when it is okay to do something.
*You **can** pay me tomorrow.*

We use *can't* when it is not okay or it is prohibited to do something.
*You **can't** eat in here.*

C Prepositions of movement

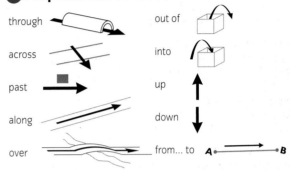

through	out of
across	into
past	up
along	down
over	from... to A — B

Module 15

A Infinitive of purpose

*I'm studying English **to get** a better job.*	(= because I want to get a better job)
*I went to the bank **to change** some money.*	(= because I wanted to change some money)

We use the infinitive (*to do, to get*) to say *why* we do things.

B *Might* and *will*: modal verbs for possibility

I/you/he/ she/you/they	'll (= Will)	go to university	(you think this will happen)
	might	go to	(you think it's
		university	possible)
	might not	go to university	(you think it's less possible)
	won't (= will not)	go to university	(you think this will not happen)

We use *might (not)* and *will (won't)* to say that something is possible or probable in the future.

> **REMEMBER**
> *We don't use to ..... after might and will.*
>
> It might rain. ~~It might to rain.~~

Irregular verbs

Verb	Past Simple	Past Participle
be	was/were	been
become	became	become
begin	began	begun
bring	brought	brought
build	built	built
buy	bought	bought
catch	caught	caught
choose	chose	chosen
come	came	come
cost	cost	cost
cut	cut	cut
do	did	done
draw	drew	drawn
drink	drank	drunk
drive	drove	driven
eat	ate	eaten
fall	fell	fallen
feed	fed	fed
feel	felt	felt
fight	fought	fought
find	found	found
fly	flew	flown
forget	forgot	forgotten
get	got	got
give	gave	given
go	went	gone/been
have	had	had
hear	heard	heard
keep	kept	kept
know	knew	known
learn	learned/learnt	learned/learnt
leave	left	left

Verb	Past Simple	Past Participle
let	let	let
lose	lost	lost
make	made	made
mean	meant	meant
meet	met	met
pay	paid	paid
put	put	put
read /riːd/	read /red/	read /red/
ring	rang	rung
run	ran	run
say	said	said
see	saw	seen
sell	sold	sold
send	sent	sent
show	showed	shown
shut	shut	shut
sit	sat	sat
sleep	slept	slept
speak	spoke	spoken
spend	spent	spent
stand	stood	stood
steal	stole	stolen
swim	swam	swum
take	took	taken
teach	taught	taught
tell	told	told
think	thought	thought
understand	understood	understood
wake	woke	woken
wear	wore	worn
win	won	won
write	wrote	written

Tapescripts

Module 1

Recording 1

A: How are you?
B: I'm fine, thanks.
C: What's your name?
D: My name's Emily Harman.
E: Where are you from?
F: I'm from England.
G: Nice to meet you.
H: And you.

Recording 3

1 A: What's his name?
   B: His name's Jarek.
   A: Where's he from?
   B: He's from Poland.
2 C: What's her name?
   D: Her name's Carmen.
   C: Where's she from?
   D: She's from Spain.
3 A: What are their names?
   B: Their names are Toshi and Mariko.
   A: Where are they from?
   B: They're from Tokyo.

Recording 4

A: His name's Jarek and he's nineteen years old. He's from Poland. He's a student at Warsaw University. He isn't married, he's single.
B: Her name's Carmen and she's from Spain. She's about thirty-five and she's married. She isn't on holiday, she's on business.
C: Their names are Toshi and Mariko. They're from Tokyo. They're tourists: and they're on holiday in Italy. They're about twenty-two and they aren't married, they're friends.

Recording 6

1 A: Are you a student?
   B: Yes, I am. I'm at London University.
   C: Where are you from?
   D: We're from Australia.
   E: How old are you?
   F: I'm 21.
   G: Are you married?
   H: Yes, we are.
   I: Are you on holiday?
   J: Yes, I am.
   K: What's your job?
   L: I'm an architect.

Recording 7

Conversation One

B = Bruno   M = Market researcher

M: Excuse me …
B: Yes?
M: Can I ask you some questions … it's for Market Research.
B: Yes, OK.
M: Thank you very much. So, the first question … how old are you? Are you 15–19? 20–24? 25–29 maybe? 30 to …
B: No I'm twenty-two …
M: Twenty two – so that's 20–24, Fine. Are you married?
B: No!
M: OK, and what's your job … are you a student?
B: No, I'm a musician …

Conversation Two

T = Taxi telephone operator   B = Bruno

T: A1 Taxis …
B: Hello. I need a taxi please …
T: OK, what's your address?
B: It's 19 A Newton Road … Leeds …
T: Nineteen A, OK … And what's your telephone number?
B: It's 903 0294.
T: 903 0294. And what's your surname?
B: Sertori.
T: Sorry? How do you spell it?
B: It's S-E-R
T: S-E-R, Yes?
B: T-O-R
T: T-O-R … Mm
B: I. Sertori.
T: OK, Mr Sertori, The taxi'll be about ten minutes …
B: Right. Goodbye.
T: Bye.

Module 2

Recording 5

A: Minnie is Mickey Mouse's girlfriend.
B: Marge is Homer's wife.
   Bart is Homer and Marge's son.
C: Noel is Liam's brother.
D: Prince William is Queen Elizabeth's grandson.
E: Princess Stephanie is Princess Caroline's sister.
F: Paul McCartney is Stella McCartney's father.
G: Obélix is Astérix's friend.

Recording 8

I = interviewer   H = Hannah

H: OK … so this is my family tree …
I: Right …
H: As you can see, I'm an only child …
I: No brothers and sisters
H: No … only me! My father's name is John … and he's forty … forty-eight? I think … yes, forty-eight.
I: 48 years old.
H: Yes, I'm sure! So that's my dad, my mother is Elaine … and she's a teacher.
I: Just like you!
H: That's right, we're both teachers … so those are my parents … now my mother has got two sisters … so I've got two aunts, Auntie Pat and Aunt Sally …
I: So what about Auntie Pat?
H: Well, she's very nice! She's my favourite aunt, really … she's married … her husband's name is Serge …
I: Serge?
H: Yes, it's not an English name … he's French, from France …

I: Oh right ... and who's Sally?

H: Sally is my other aunt ... she's the other sister ... and Sally isn't married ...

I: Okay, and these are your cousins, yeah?

H: Marc and Lily. Yeah, they're my cousins ...

I: How old are they?

H: Marc is ... he's nineteen now, he's a student ... and Lily, well, she's the baby of the family ... she's not really a baby, she's thirteen, but she's a baby to me ... she's still at school ...

Module 3

Recording 4
Life in Britain

A: Many British people live in houses, not flats. Most houses have gardens.

B: Most office workers start work at about nine in the morning and finish at about five or six in the evening. Most people don't go home for lunch.

People usually eat a big meal in the evening; they just have a snack at lunchtime.

A: Children start school at about nine, and finish at about half past three. Most children have lunch at school. All children start school when they are four or five years old, and leave when they are sixteen or eighteen.

B: Most shops open at about nine and close at about six. Usually, they don't close for lunch. Many supermarkets stay open twenty-four hours. Most pubs and restaurants close at about eleven o'clock.

Recording 7
Conversation 1

A: ... because, you see, I don't usually have breakfast ... I'm never hungry in the morning ...

B: Really? I love breakfast ... I have a really big breakfast every day! I love ...

Conversation 2

C: so anyway because I'm thirty this year I want to ...

D: Are you thirty this year? Really? Me too! It's horrible, isn't it!

Conversation 3

E: Are you married?

F: No ... how about you?

E: No, me neither ...

Conversation 4

G: What do you want to listen to ... do you like jazz?

H: No, I don't. Do you?

G: Sometimes ... I love Stan Getz.

Conversation 5

I: ...yeah, and I'm really lucky I've got a lovely flat in the city centre, just near the station ... and I live with some friends ...

J: How fantastic ... I still live with my parents ... in Kingston ... do you know where that is ...?

Conversation 6

K: So where are you from?

L: I'm from South Africa ... Durban ... you're from Argentina, aren't you?

K: Well Chile, actually ... Santiago ...

Conversation 7

M: ... because I haven't got any brothers and sisters, you see ... I'm an only child ...

N: Yeah, me too... do you like ...?

Module 4

Recording 1

A: American superstar Whitney Houston loves dogs. She has two dogs, who live in a $75,000 dog house in her garden.

B: Actress Kim Basinger doesn't like crowds: she also hates open spaces!

A: Sylvester Stallone – star of the 'Rocky' films – likes playing golf so much he sometimes stops filming for a game.

B: Hollywood actress Camaron Diaz hates TV.

A: Actor and film director Harrison Ford says he really likes doing housework!

B: Does Superman like flying? Well, actor Dean Cain – Superman in the TV series – doesn't travel by plane ... he's too nervous!

Recording 3
An American in England

B = Bob   R = Radio journalist

R: Bob Kessler is forty-two. He's a writer, and he lives in a small village in the west of England with his wife and daughter. Bob, you aren't English, are you?

B: No, I'm from West Hills, a small town in California in the United States.

R: And what's your job?

B: I write travel books, mainly about England and the English, but also about other countries like Italy and France. I go to Europe two or three times a year.

R: And what do you think of England?

B: I like it here. I don't want to go back to the United States: I like the traditions and the way of life ... it's so different from the States ... for example I love the way everyone says 'Sorry' all the time ... I don't understand why, but it's nice!

R: So you're happy in England?

B: Yes, very happy ... my daughter goes to school here and she's got lots of English friends. And you know, now my wife and I usually drink milk with our tea!

Recording 4

J, L and P= students   T = Teacher

a N: How do you say 'futebol' in English ?

   T: It's nearly the same word ... in English, we say 'football'.

   N: OK ... I always play football at the weekend.

   T: Good!

   N: How do you spell it?

   T: F–O–O–T–B–A–L–L.

b T: Luisa, can you read aloud, please?

   L: Fairburn is an industrial town in the ...

   T: Yes, Angelo?

   A: What does 'town' mean ...?

   T: A town is a small city. Do you understand?

   A: Yes. Thank you.

c T: OK ... that's the end. Have you got any questions? Yes, Pierre ...

   P: Is it correct to say 'time for going home'?

   T: Well, we usually say 'time to go home'.

   P: So ... is it time to go home?

   T: Yes!

Module 5

Recording 1

OK, so number one is an aeroplane ... then it's ... a train, a train is number two ... next is ... then it's ... well, I suppose number three is a motorbike ... and then number four is a car and a taxi, they're the same really ... so that's four and five, a car and a taxi ... and an underground train is number six ... after that number seven ... is ... a tram ... a tram or a bus? I'm not sure ... OK maybe a bus, a bus is number seven, yeah, a tram is number eight, and a scooter, I suppose then is number nine and a bicycle is last, that's number ten ...

Recording 2

Transport Facts

A: Traffic jams in Bangkok, the capital city of Thailand, are so bad that a normal journey to work takes about three hours.

B: People in most countries drive on the right ... but people drive on the left in fifty-nine countries, including Japan, India, Australia and Great Britain.

C: More than 100,000,000 (one hundred million) people in the world ride a bicycle!

A: Every day, more than one million people travel into the centre of London: 35% come in by underground, 30% take the train, 25 % travel by car, 7% catch the bus ... and 3% walk to work!

B: In Tokyo, people never wait for more than five minutes for an underground train. The only problem is that the trains are so crowded that it's difficult to get on ... or get off!

A: Fifty-three million people fly to and from O'Hare Airport in Chicago, U.S.A. every year! (That's about one hundred people every minute!)

Recording 3

C = Carl Wilson

C: I live near the city centre and we have a real problem with cars here. Most people come to work by car, so in the morning when people drive into Boston, and in the evening, it's very busy. I have a car, but I don't drive much: I'm an artist, so I usually work at home!

Recording 5

Louise

How do I go to work? Well, it's a five minute walk to the subway – station and then I take a train to my office. It takes about twenty-five minutes on the train and costs a dollar fifty.

Ara

If you want to go from Paris to San Sebastian, you can't fly direct, so you fly to Bilbao airport. That takes about one hour forty minutes. Then you take a bus from Bilbao to San Sebastian. The bus takes about one and a half hours from the airport to the centre of town.

Yuka

If you want to get from Tokyo to Disneyland, you go by train from Tokyo Station. It's very fast. It takes about twenty minutes to Maihama station and it costs about 300 yen.

Recording 6

Person A

A: Well, usually I take the underground ... and then I walk from the station to my office.

Person B

B: Yes, I do! I love riding my motorbike ... I do it every weekend.

Person C

C: No, never. I always take my car. I just don't like buses and trains ... so crowded ...

Person D

D: About ... oh, about half an hour, thirty minutes ... sometimes more ... it depends on the traffic ...

Person E

E: Well, in a normal week, I walk around ... about ten kilometres, I'd say ... I really like walking ... I walk as much as I can ...

Person F

F: Um ... yes, it's not bad ... the trams are very good ... the buses can be a bit slow, but in general, yes, it's good.

Consolidation, Modules 1–5

Recording 1

Elspeth is a really good friend of mine. She's about twenty five years old and she lives in Edinburgh, in a big flat near the city centre. She works at the Scottish Museum and her job is very important to her. She isn't married but she's got a boyfriend, Nick. They haven't got a car because they don't like driving, but they ride their bicycles all round the city. Elspeth likes going to restaurants, going to the cinema, and meeting people and she's very friendly.

Recording 2

Conversation 1

B: Hello, Irish Rail Enquiries, Anna speaking.

A: Hello. Can you give me information about trains from Belfast to Dublin?

B: When are you travelling?

A: Tomorrow. What time is the first train in the morning?

B: The first train is at ... six thirty.

A: And what time does it arrive in Dublin?

B: Eight forty.

A: How much is it?

B: Single or return?

A: Single.

B: £21

A: Thank you.

B: You're welcome.

Conversation 2

This is London Zoo. Our offices are closed at present and no officer is available. General information on the zoo follows. *pause*
The zoo is open every day from ten a.m. to five thirty p.m. Admission for adults is £10, and for children from seven to fourteen it's £8. Children under seven are free. The nearest underground station is Camden Town which is only ten minutes' walk away. If you come by ...

Conversation 3

C: What time is the football on?

D: It starts at seven.

C: And when does it finish?

D: About 9–9.30. It depends.

C: Oh no! I want to watch a film at nine o'clock!

Module 6

Recording 1

Matthew

Well, I always have breakfast at home … not too early about ten o'clock usually …I always have tea, that's very important two or three cups of tea … and a piece of toast, with butter and jam … and sometimes a bowl of cereal … that's about all, really …

Sonia

In Brazil, we have very good tropical fruit … guava, mango and things like that … and we always have fruit for our breakfast – also we have coffee, of course, everybody knows in Brazil we have very good coffee … and maybe bread and jam …

The Weber family

Well, in our family we have breakfast together in the morning when we have time … we have coffee, usually … and we have many types of bread which we have with butter and jam … and maybe some cheese, sometimes we have cheese for breakfast maybe ham as well … oh and eggs, sometimes we have eggs as well …

Recording 3

Joke 1

A: Waitress?

B: Yes, sir.

A: Can I have some ice-cream, please, one spoonful of vanilla, one scoop – no two scoops – of chocolate … three scoops of strawberry … and two scoops of banana flavour … and I'd like some chocolate sauce with it … and some cream …

B: Right sir. So that's one scoop of vanilla, two scoops of chocolate, three scoops of strawberry and two scoops of banana flavour.

A: Yes make that three scoops of banana.

B: Three scoops of banana … with chocolate sauce and cream …

A: Yes, that's right.

B: And do you want a cherry on top?

A: No thanks, I'm on a diet.

Joke 2

C: Waiter!

D: Is there a problem, sir?

C: Yes, there is a problem! There's a fly in my soup!

D: Oh … Can I see, sir … oh yes, you're right … Do you want a knife and fork, sir?

Joke 3

E: Waiter?

D: Yes, sir.

E: I have a question. What's in the Chicken Surprise Pie?

D: Chicken, sir.

E: Chicken? … so what's the surprise?

D: The chicken's got feathers, sir.

Recording 4

A: Waiter! Waiter!

B: Yes, sir?

A: There's a spider in my soup!

B: Really, sir? Can I see?

A: Look! There it is!

B: Oh, I see. Yes, you're right sir. The fly is on holiday.

Recording 5

Conversation 1

A: Can I take your order, please?

B: Yes, can I have two Super King Size Burgers, please.

A: Two Super King Size, yeah

B: With large fries …

A: Anything to drink with that?

B: Yes, a coke and a lemonade please

A: Eat in or take away?

B: Sorry?

A: Do you want it to eat here or take away?

B: Oh, eat here, please,

A: Right that's £8.50, please.

Conversation 2

A: Would you like anything else? Some more coffee?

B: No thanks. Can I have the bill, please?

A: OK so it's just one coffee … and piece of chocolate cake

B: That's right.

A: So that's £1.45 for the coffee and £1.35 for the cake.

A: That's £2.80 altogether, please.

B: £2.80 … one, two, three pounds … there you are. Keep the change.

A: Oh.Thank you..

B: That's all right. Bye bye.

A: Bye.

Conversation 3

A: Perfect Pizza, good evening.

B: Yes, I'd like to order a pizza … to be delivered, please.

A: All right … what would you like?

B: The one with all the different kinds of cheese … and ham … I haven't got a menu, what's the name of it?

A: Right, that's the Cheese Supreme.

B: That's it.

A: And is that regular, large, or extra large?

B: How much is the extra large?

A: The regular is £7.60, the large is £10.60, and the extra large is £12.60.

B: Oh … the large Cheese Supreme please

A: Anything else?

B: Yeah, a litre bottle of Diet Lemonade, please.

A: Right …

B: How much is that altogether?

A: That's 10.60 for the pizza, 1.25 for the drink so that's … 11.85 altogether.

B: Okay

A: All right, what's the address?

B: It's 28 Southlands Road …

Recording 6

There's a man in the picture … and two women.

Well, the man has got something in his hand … in his right hand yes, he's got a paper bag in his right hand.

I think his name's Frank, because there's a sign at the back which says 'Frank's Fruit and Veg'

I can see a cat … it's a black cat … on the right.

There are lots of fruit and vegetables on the left of the picture. Let's see … there are some potatoes … they're 54 pence a kilo …

Then there are some grapes … they're £1.53 pence a kilo …

The next fruit is apples, there are only four apples, as well … and the sign says 'Apples £1.09 a kilo.

There's also a sign that says 'bananas' … but there's a problem … because there aren't any … there are no bananas in the box …

Module 7

Recording 5

I only knew my great-grandfather for a few years ..His name was George, and he died when I was about ten … but he certainly had a very interesting life! He was born in a small village in Poland I'm not sure when, some time in the 1920s, I think – and he lived there in this village until 1940, when the Second World War began. And when the soldiers came, he decided to leave Poland – he wanted to join the British Army, so do you know what he did? He walked all the way from his village in Poland to Egypt … it took him about three months, incredible! When the war ended he went to live in England … where he met my great-grandmother, who was also Polish and they got married. They lived in England for the next fifty years … they always spoke Polish at home, though.

Recording 7

Extract A

I was born in 1978 … in a place called Swansea, which is a town in the south of Wales … my mum and dad were very happy, I think … I was their first daughter.

Extract B

I became interested in music when I was very, very young, I always loved music … when I was about three or four, I got a piano … not a real one, a toy piano, for Christmas … and I just loved it … I played with it for hours.

Extract C

I went to school in Swansea … I was happy at school most of the time … music was my favourite subject … of course!

Extract D

When I was about twelve, I began to have piano lessons my mum and Dad got a teacher for me, and I learned how to play the piano it was quite difficult, but I enjoyed it.

Extract E

I went to University in Wales I'm sure you know what I studied … it was Music and Drama, and I graduated in 1999 …

Extract F

Last year I became a professional singer … I made my first CD … I sang on a CD by someone called Hugh Morris … it was really exciting …

Module 8

Recording 2

A: In the story, Tarzan lived in the African jungle: one day he met a girl called Jane and they fell in love! But Tarzan didn't ride a motorbike!

B: In the old story, Robin Hood lived in a forest, he always wore green clothes and he took money from rich people: but he didn't give it to Maid Marian! He gave money to poor people.

C: The story is that Count Dracula slept during the day, and that at night he became a bat and drank blood … but he didn't live in a castle in Brazil; he lived in Transylvania, in central Europe.

Recording 4

M = tour guide   B = little boy

M: … and here we are at the castle. There is a story that many, many years ago a dragon lived here in our town …

B: Did the dragon live in this house?

M: No, he didn't. He lived in a cave. So, there was a terrible dragon, and the people of the town were very sad … because, well, the dragon ate all the young girls of the town …

B: Did the dragon eat boys?

M: No, no he didn't. Only girls. So, one day, a prince came to the town and …

B: Did the prince have a girlfriend?

M: Er … I don't know … so the prince decided to do something, and one day …

B: Did the prince kill the dragon?

M: Yes, he did.

B: How?

M: Well, it was rather difficult to kill the dragon, so what he did was …

Recording 6

A = interviewer   B = female writer

A: So, Tina, what's the title of your very short story?

B: The name of the story is 'Charlie Who?' – they're not in the sixty words, though!

A: And how long did it take you to write it?

B: I wrote it one afternoon … it didn't take a long time to write … about an hour, I think.

A: Who are your favourite writers?

B: That's a difficult question! I don't have a favourite really … I read everything!!

A: So, where did you get the idea for the story?

B: I read something in the newspaper about a man who won the lottery … and he had a party for everyone in his street. That gave me the idea.

A: And what's the story about?

B: Well, as I said it's about a man called Charlie … but it's also about money … and how people think about money.

A: Did you expect to win the competition?

B: No, I didn't. It was a complete surprise!

Recording 7

Charlie bought a lottery ticket with a £1 coin: his last. The next day he won £10 million. Charlie gave a party for his neighbours – it lasted two weeks. On the last day, Charlie died. The government took all his money, but everyone in the street always remembered the incredible street party. But they couldn't remember who gave it.

Recording 8

René woke up as usual at half past nine. He looked out of the window. It was another beautiful day in Monte Carlo. He went downstairs and had his usual breakfast: espresso coffee and three oranges. Before he finished his meal, the phone rang. He answered it. 'Hello?' Silence. Then… 'René?' A woman's voice: he knew it immediately. It was Sylvia, his ex-girlfriend.
'Yes.' he answered. 'Thank Goodness it's you, René. I've got a problem, and I need your help. Meet me in one hour.'
René left the apartment, got into his car and drove to the car park of the Grand Casino. He arrived at a quarter to eleven. She wasn't there. René looked at his watch.
Suddenly René saw someone, but it wasn't Sylvia; it was a man – a very tall man, and he didn't look friendly.
There was one important question in René's mind: 'Where's the money?' he asked.
'Sylvia's got it' the tall man answered. 'Come with me.'
René went with the tall man. He followed him to a car. It was a very big black car. He got into the back of the car and saw a woman. She had a big bag. It was the money …
'Thank Goodness it's you, Sylvia. Are you OK?
'Me?' She answered slowly. 'Oh yes. I'm fine. But you are not fine. You are in big trouble. This is a police car and you are going to prison.'

Module 9

Recording 2

Carla
Well, the best food in the world comes from Italy – in my opinion – and I suppose the most famous food from Italy is pasta, so it's a good idea to buy some pasta … and maybe some sauce or olive oil to go with it … delicious …

Helena
My country is very famous for music … especially samba music … I think a CD of typical samba music from Brazil is a very good souvenir.

Greg
If you like books, you can buy a book by a Polish writer, her name is Wisława Szymborska. She won the Nobel Prize for Literature … You can buy an English translation if you don't know Polish!

Guy
A good thing to buy is a bottle of wine, French wine is famous all around the world and the best wine comes from Bordeaux, in southwest France …

Recording 3

1 A: Do you sell toothpaste?
  B: No, we don't. Try the pharmacy.

2 A: Do you accept credit cards?
  C: Yes, Visa or Mastercard.

3 A: Have you got this in a smaller size?
  D: Let me check for you.

4 A: How much is this?
  E: It's £25

5 A: What time do you close?
  F: At eight o'clock.

6 A: Can I have one of those, please?
  G: This one?

Recording 4

1 A: How much are these postcards?
  B: Twenty-five pence each. How many have you got?
  A: Eight.
  B: That's two pounds.
  A: And I'd like eight stamps for Canada.
  B: That's four pounds altogether.
2 A: Do you sell batteries?
  C: Yes, what size?
  A: It's for this camera.
  C: Let me see. OK. How many do you want?
  A: Two, please.
  C: That's two pounds.
3 A: How much is this tee-shirt?
  E: It's £19.99
  A: Have you got it in a smaller size?
  E: Let me check for you. Yes, I've got one here.
  A: Okay, I'll have it. Do you accept credit cards?
  E: Visa or Mastercard. Can you sign here. Thank you.
4 A: Can I have one of those cakes, please?
  F: This one?
  A: No, that one, there.
  F: Anything else?

A: Yes, some bread please.
F: Medium or small?
A: Small please.
F: That's £1.20

Module 10

Recording 1

D: Hello.
J: Hello Dan, where are you?
D: I'm in King Street – just outside the Post Office.
J: What are you doing?
D: I'm waiting for a bus … how are you?
J: I'm fine.

Recording 2

Michelle
Generally, I really like my uniform – its' smart. I wear a white shirt, a black jacket , black trousers or skirt, a kind of back and white shirt, and this lovely black hat (laughing)! There's only one thing that I hate … the shoes! Police shoes are really big and ugly … yuk!

Andy
Our uniforms are interesting because they're very very old. Imagine … the hats we wear are more than 300 years old. People were smaller then, so the uniforms are really uncomfortable now, and very heavy – you want to move your head all the time, but you can't of course. The trousers are also old, and they are made of a special kind of leather – also very uncomfortable, so we wear women's tights under them. We don't usually tell people about that, though!

Recording 3

This is a picture of a street. It's a lovely morning and the sun is shining. On the left of the picture there is a girl is walking along the street. She's wearing a white skirt and she's listening to some music on her headphones.
In the middle of the picture there's a man with a big black and white dog: the dog is running after a cat. The dog's owner is wearing a pair of sunglasses.
On the right of the picture, there are two women sitting at a table and drinking coffee. One of the women has got short dark hair. She is tall, slim and beautiful.

Recording 4

a A: Excuse me, have you got the time, please?
  B: Yes, it's ten o'clock.
b C: Is this seat free?
  D: Sure, take it.
c E: Is this bus going to the city centre?
  F: Yes, that's right.
d G: Is it OK to smoke here?
  H: I'm sorry, it's a non smoking area.
e I: Excuse me … how do I get to the railway station?
    Sorry, I don't live here.

Consolidation Modules 6–10

Recording 1
a   Can I have the bill please?
b   How much is this tee-shirt?
c   I'd like to order two large pizzas, please.
d   I'm sorry, I don't understand. Can you say it again please?
e   Do you sell shampoo?
f   Have you got this in a bigger size?
g   No, thanks, I'm just looking.

Module 11

Recording 1
Cats started living with people as pets thousands of years ago, and now there are about 500 million domestic cats around the world. Cats are usually very good hunters and can catch mice and small birds – although they often don't eat them, if they can get normal cat food! In fact, they are very lazy animals: on average, they sleep for about sixteen hours a day. They also spend a lot of time keeping themselves clean by washing their fur with their tongues.
Male cats are called toms and female cats are called queens: female cats are pregnant for about nine weeks, and usually have between two and five kittens. There are over one hundred breeds of cat, and even a hairless cat called the sphynx cat!

Recording 2
RADIO JOURNALIST: People say that a dog is a man's best friend. People and dogs first started living together about ten thousand years ago. Now there are fifty-three million dogs just in the U.S.A. – the Americans spend over two billion dollars on dog food every year – four times what they spend on baby food! Altogether there are about a hundred and fifty breeds of dog. Many dogs work for humans, doing jobs such as helping the blind, helping the police and customs officers to find drugs, and even racing! Greyhound racing is popular in many countries. The fastest greyhounds can run as fast as 65 kilometres per hour. Perhaps the most famous working dog was called Rin Tin Tin, who died in 1932. He earned his money by making films – he made fifty films and earned about forty-four thousand dollars for each one!

Recording 3
1   Which language or languages do people speak in Canada?
2   Where was the Hollywood actor Arnold Schwarzenegger born?
3   How many players are there in a basketball team?
4   How long does it take to boil an egg?
5   When did Bill Clinton become President of the United States?
6   Which is the biggest desert in the world?
7   When did Joseph Niépce invent the first camera?
8   How far is it from the Earth to the Moon?
9   When did France win the World Cup in football?
10 Sushi is a popular type of food. Where does it come from?

Recording 4
1   Canada has two official languages: French, which is spoken by about 40% of the population, and English, which is spoken by the remaining 60%.
2   Although he has lived in the United States for many years, the popular Hollywood actor and director Arnold Schwarzenegger was born in Graz, a city in Austria, in 1947.
3   A basketball team has five players.

4   There are several different methods of boiling an egg: but most cooks agree that it should take between three and four minutes, depending on whether you like your egg hard or soft.
5   Bill Clinton first became President of the United States in 1992. He won a second election in 1996.
6   With an area of nearly eight and a half million square kilometres, the Sahara is the largest desert in the world.
7   A Frenchman named Joseph Niépce invented the camera in 1826. It took him eight hours to take the first photograph!
8   The distance from the Earth to the Moon is approximately 380,000 kilometres.
9   France won the World Cup for the first time in 1998. They beat Brazil 3–0 in the final in Paris.
10 Sushi is a type of food made from fish which is raw – or not cooked. It is most commonly eaten in Japan.

Module 12

Recording 1
Tania
Tania, 18: On Saturday night I'm going out with a big group of people … probably to a club, because it's one of my friend's birthday … then on Sunday I'm going with the whole family to my grandparents' house for lunch …

Amir
Amir, 25: I'm quite tired, so I'm not going to do much this weekend … just have a quiet time at home. I want to finish the book I'm reading and sleep lots!

Phil
Phil, 33: I'd like to go away somewhere this weekend – maybe go walking in the country – but it depends on the weather …

Aphra
Aphra, 28: It's my boyfriend's birthday on Sunday... so on Saturday, I'm going shopping to buy his present … I'd like to get him a new watch if I can find a nice one, then on Sunday I'm going to cook a special birthday meal for him.

Zoe
Zoe, 20: I've got to work on Saturday … so that's Saturday … I don't know about Sunday … sleep probably …

Val
Val, 46: I'm going on holiday on Sunday – to South Africa – so tomorrow I'm going to pack … and iron … and do all the jobs I need to do before I go away …

Recording 4
Conversation A
OW = older woman   YW = younger woman
OW: Let's stop for a break – this is really tiring!
YW: Good idea – shall I make some coffee?
OW: It's OK, I'll make it
YW: No, I'll make it – you sit down.
OW: OK then … thanks …

Conversation B
W = woman   M = man
W: I'm really bored, shall we go out somewhere tonight?
M: Yes fine, what do you want to do?
W: We could go and see a film …
M: OK then – but which film?
W: How about that new one with Julia Roberts? I can't remember the name of it.

M: OK, if you like …

W: Shall I find out when it's on, and what time it starts?

M: Yes, good idea …

Recording 5

C = Craig   R = Ruth   B = Betsy

R: What are you doing on Sunday, anything interesting?

C: Nothing much.

B: Me neither.

R: Perhaps we could go somewhere together …why don't we have a day out, we're always saying we're: going to, but we never do …

B: Yeah but where?

R: I'd like to go to Lyme Regis – everyone says it's lovely …

C: Yes, it is, but it's a long way … it takes about three hours to get there … better for a weekend than: just one day …

B: Or how about Bath … that's great, and there are lovely shops …

C: But again, it's quite a long way …

B: Yeah, I suppose so …

B: I know – how about Leeds Castle? I'd love to go there, it looks so beautiful in photographs: and it's not too far …

C: Yeah, I'd really like to go there too … there are lovely walks, people say.

R: OK then … but what about transport? Can you get the train there?

B: Don't worry about that – I can borrow the car – I'll drive us there …

R: Oh brilliant – well let's go there then …

C: The only thing is, I think it's quite expensive to get in … and then if we have to pay for lunch and

R: Well let's take a picnic … then we won't spend money on lunch

B: Yeah, good idea …

R: I'll make it … what shall we have – sandwiches? fruit? crisps? sausages?

C: Yeah, great, and I'll get some drinks … lemonade and coke and things …

B: Okay then … so what time shall I pick you up?

C: Not too early, about eleven o'clock?

R: The only problem is that I need to be home quite early – I've got some work to do before Monday: morning …

B: Okay then, well let's leave at about ten o'clock then, and then we can be back about half past six – is that okay for everyone?

R: Yeah perfect.

C: Great … it'll be great …

Recording 7

Everybody thinks that in Canada it's always cold, and in the north, in the Yukon Territory it's true; there's snow maybe eight months of the year. But I come from Vancouver, on the west coast, and there the winters aren't too bad. Most days it's cloudy and it can be quite wet sometimes, but it's not really cold. The summers are nice: it's quite sunny and warm – I guess the average is about eighteen degrees.
In the Prairies – that's the central part of the country – it gets very hot in summer. In the winter it's very windy because of a wind we call the 'chinook'. It can be a problem for the farmers, as it doesn't rain very much. In the eastern part of the country …

Module 13

Recording 1

One day, Marty went out to buy a newspaper. He saw a competition in the newspaper and decided to enter: Marty loved competitions. There was a simple question to answer:
Where do koalas live?
First, he told the man next door about the competition, and asked if he knew the answer: but the man didn't know, so Marty looked in a

book.
A few days later, a letter came through the door. Marty opened the letter excitedly … inside there was a piece of paper … a cheque for £1,000!!
Then he looked at the name on the envelope. He saw that the letter wasn't for him: it was for the man next door.

Recording 2

J = Jane

Conversation 1

J: Hello, can I speak to Paul, please?

A: Sorry, he's not here

J: Oh, I see … do you know when he'll be back

A: Not really, no …

J: OK, I'll try again this afternoon:

A: OK, 'bye.

Conversation 2

B = woman in Travel agent

B: TKO Travel, good morning

J: Hello, is that Julia Thomson?

B: Speaking.

J: Hello, this is Jane Hancock, I'm ringing about the flight tickets …

B: Oh, right yes …

J: … for Copenhagen. Are they ready yet ?

J: Yes, well unfortunately there's a bit of a problem Ö

Conversation 3

AM = answer machine   J = Jane

AM: Hello, this is Tania Shaw… Sorry, I'm not here at the moment. Please leave a message after the tone:

:BEEP:

J: Hi, it's Jane here, can you phone me back ? It's about the flight tickets. My number is 890921. Talk to you soon. Bye!

Conversation 4

M = Jane's mum

M: Hello?

J: Hello, Mum, it's me. Is Dad there?

M: He's asleep in front of the television. Shall I wake him up?

J: No, it's okay. Can you ask him to phone me?

M: Yes, of course. Is everything okay

J: Oh yes, I'm fine I've just got to do all these things before Saturday

Module 14

Recording 1

Postcard 1

OK, so these are all pictures of my city, which is Budapest, in Hungary … and in the picture there's a bridge, the name of this bridge is 'Elizabeth Bridge' … it's one of the most famous bridges over the River Danube … also you can see Váci Utca … or Váci Street … there are no cars there, it's a pedestrian street, full of fashionable shops … also you can see a castle, … and the famous Heroes' Square …

Postcard 2

Here you can see some of the most famous sights of Rio de Janeiro in Brazil. It's not the capital – that's Brasilia – but for me, it's the most beautiful city … there's a picture of the Maracaná Stadium, the famous sports stadium, it's maybe the most famous football stadium in the world, Maracaná, we can also see the famous beach at Copacabana and of course you have the famous statue of Christ, which you can see from all over the city it's on a hill called Corcovado …

Recording 4

As your train moves out of the little railway station at St Moritz, prepare yourself for a day to remember! The journey from the ski resort of St Moritz to the attractive town of Zermatt in central Switzerland is only 290 km: but on the way it passes through some of the most beautiful scenery in Europe. During its journey, the train goes through 91 tunnels, and travels over nearly 300 bridges … if you don't like heights, don't look down when you travel over the Oberalp Pass: the track is nearly 2,000m high! As you look out of the train window, you can see some of Switzerland's most fantastic mountains … the train goes past mountains like the famous Jungfrau. And as your train comes into the station at Zermatt, if you look up, you will see the Matterhorn – Switzerland's highest mountain.

Recording 5

… and if you look up, on the right hand-side of the bus you have a very good view of Edinburgh castle at the top of the hill … the oldest part of the building – St. Margaret's Chapel – is nearly 900 years old, and the castle as a whole has been occupied since at least … *fade*
We are now driving along the street known as the Royal Mile … this is one of the oldest streets – and at 1.6 kilometres, the longest in Edinburgh … as you can see, there are many historic houses in the street, and many cafés, bars and restaurants here where you can relax over a drink and … *fade*
The very old house on your left is John Knox's house. Approximately 500 years old, it is the oldest house in the Royal Mile, and one of the oldest in Scotland … it is where John Knox – the religious reformer who lived in Edinburgh – died in 1572. Knox was well-known in his time for …
The fine neo-classical building which contains about four thousand paintings, not only by Scottish painters, but also by well-known European painters such as the Italian master Titian. The gallery is open every day from nine o'clock …
… and opposite Holyrood Palace you can see the Our Dynamic Earth Exhibition, which shows the history of Planet Earth with a variety of the latest hi-technology displays. It opened for the first time in July 1999 and a family ticket costs £20.00 for two adults and three children … *fade*

Recording 6

… right … let's see … probably the best way is … go along this road … over South Bridge there … and carry on for about 500 metres until the end of this road, North Bridge … when you come to the Tourist Information Centre on the corner … turn left into Princes Street … go straight on for about 500 metres … past the market and the Scott Monument on your left … and just before the Floral Clock turn left, that street's called the Mound … you go straight on … and the Art Gallery is on your left – it's the second big building on your left …
How long does it take?
Probably about 20 minutes.
OK, thank you.
Pleasure.

Module 15

Recording 2
Francine
Languages were always my favourite subjects at school. When I was at primary school where they taught us French from the age of eight … I found the lessons interesting, and I soon found that I was good at learning languages … so then I started learning Spanish as well. Now I'm at university … next year I'm going to Lisbon to study Portuguese … when I graduate, Iíd like to look for a job where I can use my languages … in an international company maybe.

Bill
I was always very bad at school. I failed all my exams, and I left secondary school at the age of 16. I'm really sorry I didn't work harder at school. I worked as a van driver for a few years … then I went to College to get some qualifications. I did a course in Information Technology. I studied in the evenings after work: for the first time I really enjoyed going to class: I took my exams again and this time I passed! It shows that it's never too late to learn. Now I've got my own computer sales company!

Recording 3
Part A
Well we can't really say that one language is easier or more difficult than another language … it depends.in some ways, yes, English is an easy language to learn … take the verbs for example … now in some languages, you have to make many, many changes to the verb – in Latin, for example, there are 120 different forms of one verb! In English, there are only five … with the verb 'go' for example, there's 'go', 'goes', 'went', 'going' and 'gone' … but we use these forms in a lot of different ways! And the spelling and pronunciation of English are more difficult than in many languages … we have a lot of sounds in English … and the spelling isn't very regular.

Part B
Well, nobody knows exactly how many people are learning English in the world today … but it's certainly more than it was 50 years ago … For example, fifty years ago very few people in China learned English, but now the number of people learning English in China is bigger than the population of the United States! So there are probably about 300 million people learning English at the moment,. which is more than any other language … and some experts say that by the year 2050 – that's about fifty years from now – half of the world's population will speak English … I'm not sure, I think we'll have to wait and see …

Recording 4
Clara
At first I thought about the Sports Studies Course because I really enjoy swimming and football, but in the end I decided that the Leisure and Tourism course is better for me. You see I like meeting people and I'd really like to work abroad for a few years, maybe as a tour guide or in a hotel, maybe in Spain.

Taka
I'd really like to do a course in art because I'm very interested in art, but I have to think about my job. I work as a fashion designer and when I go back to Japan I want to use a computer to design clothes, so I'm going to do the Basic Information Technology Course. I can study art and photography in my free time!

Ben
Yeah, well, I want to have a good time at college, you know, meet lots of people and I don't want to work too much! I like computers a lot and I might do a job with computers one day in the future, but at the moment I'm really interested in music, you know, I'm in a rock band. So I've decided to do the Performing Arts Course. Then in the first year I can do drama and music and in the second year I'll probably do a course in singing. Then me and my friends in the band can be rich and famous!

Author acknowledgements

We would like to thank the following people for their help and contribution: Andy Connor, Tessa Lochowski, Matthew Moor and Tanya Whatling. We would also like to thank everyone at Pearson Education for all their input, support and encouragement, in particular Frances Woodward (Senior Publisher), Jo Stevenson (Senior Designer), Judith Walters (Senior Editor), Alma Gray (Producer), Andrew Thorpe (Mac Artist)

The publishers and authors are very grateful to the following people and institutions for reporting on the manuscript: Károlyné Abraham, Budapest; Cristina Anastasiadis, IH Zurbano, Madrid; Fernando Armesto, Links, Buenos Aires; Annamaria Bergamini, Milan; Tom Bradbury, London School of English; Juilia Brannon, Edwards Language School, London; Rosaria Campana, Milan; Pauline Carr, Milan; John Clarke, British Council, Milan; Lynda Fletcher, Crawley College; Yvonne Gobert, Paris; Ana Gutiérrez, EOI San Blás, Madrid; Lisa Hale, St Giles, London; Alison Knowles, IH Buenos Aires; Giulia Korwin, Milan; Nora Krishmar, Links, Buenos Aires; Juarez Lopes, British House, Pelotas, Brazil; Mark Lloyd, IH Serrano, Madrid; Katie Mann, Crawley College; Sue Messenger, Crawley College; Katarzyna Niedźwiecka, Łódz; Francine Pens, EF International School of English, London; Carol Perry, EOI Porta Morera, Alicante; Elżbieta Rodzeń-Leśnikowska, Łódz; Ana Szabo, Cultura Inglesa, São Carlo; Márta Szálká, Toldi Ferrenc Gimnazium, Budapest; Alice Szamandone, Budapest; Lyanne Szartimay, Budapest; Arek Tkacz, Łódz; Monica Zafaroni, Links, Buenos Aires.

We are grateful to the following for permission to reproduce copyright material:
Carlin Music Corporation, London NW1 8BD for lyrics of 'Return to Sender' words and music by Otis Blackwell & Winfield Scott © 1962 by Elvis Presley Music Inc – all rights administered by R & H Music – all rights reserved; International Music Publications Limited for lyrics of 'Trains and Boats and Planes' words by Hal David and music by Burt Bacharach © 1964 New Hidden Valley Music and Casa David Music, USA, Warner/Chappell Music Ltd, London W6 8BS

Illustrated by: Melanie Barnes, Philip Bannister, Kathy Baxendale, Emma Brownjohn (New Division), Jessie Eckel (New Division), Melvyn Evans (New Division), Martina Farrow (New Division), Diane Fawcett (Artist Partners), Rebecca Gibbon (The Inkshed), Robert Nelmes (The Organisation), David Pattison, Gavin Reece (New Division), David Smith (The Organisation), Marcus Wilde (Three Blind Mice), Moira Wills (New Division).

Photo acknowledgements

We are grateful to the following for permission to reproduce copyright photographs:
ACE Photo Agency/Jason Burns for page 35 (bottom right), /Jigsaw for page 33 (bottom); Action Images for page 9 (5); All Action/Paul Smith for page 57 (e); Animals Unlimited for page 93 (bottom right); Aquarius, London for page 57 (h); Aspect Picture Library/J. Alex Langley for page 118 (b). /Brian Seed for page 104 (d); Associated Press for pages 58, 75 (top left); Bridgeman Art Library/Mozart Museum, Salzburg, Austria for page 61 (bottom); Britstock-IFA for page 24 (middle right), /Esbin Anderson for page 10 (1), /Eric Bach for page 53 (1), /Roger Cracknell for page 34 (top right), /M. Gottschalk for pages 114 (2 top right), 138 (lower middle right), /Walsh for page 118 (a); Camera Press for page 134 (bottom right), /William Conran for page 139 (bottom right), /Richard Open for page 9 (6), /Richard Stonehouse for page 21 (e), /Theodore Wood for page 31 (middle left); Bruce Coleman Collection/Adriano Bacchella for page 93 (top left), /Pacific Stock for page 91 (l), /Hans Reinhard for page 93 (top right), 93 (bottom left); Colorific!/Paul Conklin for page 114 (1 top right); Corbis/James L. Amos for page 96 (bottom), /Bettman for page 56 (c), 56 (f), /David Lees for page 108 (r), /George Lepp for page 91 (h), /Francis G. Mayer for page 75 (bottom left), /Neil Miller/Papilio for page 102 (a), /Minnesota Historical Society for page 59 (left), /Vince Streano for page 24 (bottom left), /Underwood & Underwood for page 59 (right), /Bob Winsett for page 19 (lower middle); James Davis for page 114 (1 left); Dorling Kindersley for page 50; Greg Evans International for pages 26 (left), 72, 77 (top right), 90 (c), 118 (f); Eye Ubiquitous/Antonio Aiello for page 125 (lower middle right); Famous/Norbert Ivanek for page 75 (bottom right); Focus PR for page 74 (2 left); Tim Graham for page 20 (c); Ronald Grant Archive for pages 31 (bottom left), 65 (1), 65 (2), 65 (3),

65 (5), 66 (a), 66 (b), /20th Century Fox for page 21 (f), /1992 Universal City Studios & Amblin for page 65 (6); Robert Harding Picture Library/N. Blythe for page 138 (top left), /C. Bowman for pages 102-103 (c), /Rolf Richardson for page 118 (c), /Peter Scholey for page 77 (lower middle right), /Noble Stock for page 105; Michael Holford for page 94 (top left); Image Bank for page 104 (a), /T. Anderson for page 45 (right), /L.D. Gordon for pages 79 (top left), 128 (top left), /Juan Silva for page 8; Images Colour Library for pages 102 (b), 104 (c), 108 (bottom middle), 125 (bottom right), 130; Impact/Giles Barnard for page 49 (top), /Anthony Taylor for page 29 (top left); Katz/Adrian Kool for page 26 (right); Kobal Collection for page 66 (c); Tessa Lochowski for page 60; London Features International for page 61 (top); Longman/by Peter Lake for pages 9 (3), 9 (8), 9 (9), 13, 24 (top left), 49 (bottom), 53 (2), 68 (middle), 78, 84 (right), 85, 87, 99 (top), 108 (l), 125 (top); Moviestore Collection for page 56 (b); NHPA/A.N.T. for page 90 (a), /N.A. Callow for page 90 (f), /Andy Rouse for page 90 (e), /A. Warburton & S. Toon for page 91 (d); Network/Gideon Mendel for page 118 (d), /Mark Peterson/SABA for page 53 (3), /Harriet Logan for page 19 (upper middle); Oxford Scientific Films/Niall Benvie for page 90 (b), /David Cayless for page 90 (g), /Peter Hawkey/Survival Anglia for page 91 (i); The Photographers Library for pages 19 (bottom), 22 (c), 22 (f), 45 (left), 74 (1 right), 74 (2 right), 74 (4 left), 74 (4 right), 79 (bottom right), 91 (i), 91 (k), 91 (n), 118 (e), 123 (bottom), 138 (bottom right); Photostage/Donald Cooper for page 128 (bottom right); Pictor International for pages 14 (bottom right), 23 (e), 24 (top right), 29 (top right), 42, 43 (top), 43 (bottom), 91 (m), 125 (middle left), 125 (upper middle right), 138 (bottom left); Pictures/Clive Sawyer for page 27; Popperfoto for pages 9 (1), 138 (upper bottom left), /Pierre Virot Reuters for page 74 (1 left), /Vision\A-100 for page 84 (middle); Redferns for page 56 (g); Retna/Adrian Boot for page 57 (d), /Bill Davila for page 75 (top right), /Ed Geller for page 31 (middle right), /John Kelly for page 31 (top right), /Mitchell Layton for page 136 (bottom right), /Photofest for pages 20 (b), 57 (a), 65 (4), 131; Rex Features for pages 9 (2), 20 (a), 21 (g), 31 (bottom right), /ABACA for page 140 (top), /Dave Lewis for page 31 (top left), /Pierre Villard/Sipa for page 20 (a); Spectrum Colour Library for pages 10 (2), 114 (1 bottom right), 138 (upper middle right); Sporting Pictures for page 9 (4); The Stock market for pages 37 (bottom right), 39 (c), 39 (e), 39 (h), 138 (lower top middle), 140 (bottom), /Georgina Bowater for page 39 (i), /Charles Gupton for page 39 (a), /David Lawrence for page 39 (b), /1999 Rob Lewine for page 79 (top right), /95 Mugshots for page 128 (top right); gettyone Stone/Glen Allison for page 138 (top right), /Brian Bailey for page 49 (middle), /Ken Biggs for pages 41 (left), 94 (bottom right), /Dan Bosler for page 34 (top left), /Stewart Cohen for pages 15 (top right), 134 (middle), 134 (bottom left), /Donna Day for page 35 (top left), /Ary Diesendruck for page 114 (2 bottom), /Laurence Dutton for page 123 (top), /Fisher/Thatcher for pages 10 (3), 79 (bottom left), 128 (middle left), /Lorentz Gullachsen for page 33 (top), /Frank Herholdt for page 70, /Dale Higgins for page 41 (middle), /Walter Hodges for page 128 (middle right), /Silvestre Machado for page 114 (2 top left), /Ranald Mackechnie for page 22 (d), /Simon McComb for pages 15 (top left), 35 (bottom left), 133, /Dave Nagel for page 128 (bottom left), /Mervyn Rees for page 138 (lower middle left), /Lorne Resnick for page 39 (f), /Charles Sleicher for page 77 (bottom right), /Brooke Slezak for pages 37 (top left), 139 (middle right), /Zeynep Sumen for page 77 (left), /Jerome Tisne for page 22 (a), /Terry Vine for page 128 (upper middle right), /John Warden for page 104 (b), /David Young-Wolff for page 35 (top right); Superstock for pages 9 (7), 36 (bottom), 37 (top right), 39 (d), 113, 139 (top right); Swatch AG/Foto Schlaefli for page 74 (3 left); Telegraph Colour Library for pages 19 (top), 22 (bottom left), 24 (bottom right), 25, 29 (middle), 69, 128 (lower middle right), /Heimo Aga for page 39 (g), /Walter Bibikow for page 41 (right), /Denis Boissary for page 23 (g), /Gary Buss for page 43 (middle), /R. Chapple for page 94 (top right), /Bill Losh for pages 37 (bottom left), 140 (middle), /Matassa for page 138 (upper middle left), /J.P. Nacivet for page 94 (bottom left), /Simon Potter for page 22 (b), /Travel Pix for page 138 (lower top left), /Jochem D. Wijnands for page 77 (upper middle right); Topham Picturepoint for pages 61 (middle), 74 (3 right), /Associated Press for page 125 (bottom left), /Press Association for pages 96 (middle), /Joe Sohm/The Image Works for page 96 (top); Trip/H. Rogers for page 36 (top); John Walmsley for page 26 (middle).

Cover photograph: Telegraph Colour Library

Special thanks to the following for their help during location photography;
Boardmans, Bishops Stortford; Pearsons Ltd., Bishops Stortford.

Freelance picture research and commissioned photography by Ann Thomson.